THE CREATIVE BOOK OF

Dolls

THE CREATIVE BOOK OF

Dolls

Jane Gisby

a Salamander book

Published by Salamander Books Limited
LONDON • NEW YORK

Published by Salamander books Ltd.,
52 Bedford Row,
London WC1R 4LR,
England.

© Salamander Books Ltd 1989

0 86101 459 6

Distributed by Hodder and Stoughton Services,
PO Box 6, Mill Road, Dunton Green,
Sevenoaks, Kent TN13 2XX.

CREDITS

Editors: Jo Finnis; Judith Casey
Designers: Glynis Edwards; Philip Gorton
Photographer: Steve Tanner
Pattern artwork: John Hutchinson
Typeset by: Flair plan Ltd, England
Colour origination by: Bantam Litho Ltd., England
Printed in Belgium by: Proost International Book Production

CONTENTS

INTRODUCTION

Creating soft doll characters can give a great deal of fun and pleasure to both the maker and the recipient of the final article.

The dolls featured in this book range from gifts for children to fund-raising items for sale in a bazaar; from decorative models worthy of permanent display to mascots for a student's room. But please remember that you do not have to follow every given detail for a particular doll. A different hair style, features or clothes will make a doll which is truly your own creation. A child can draw a doll's face to a given size, which will have great appeal. You can then paint or embroider these features.

Some knowledge of simple sewing is helpful but not essential. The opening pages of this book contain important information on the equipment, materials and sewing techniques used, which will be helpful to the beginner and may provide new tips for the experienced needleworker. Do read them before you begin to make. Following these pages are patterns and easy-to-follow step-by-step instructions and photographs to make 27 dolls in various sizes and materials.

This is a book which will encourage even the most cautious as well as the most knowledgeable to enjoy making dolls. There is much to delight the eye and hand.

EQUIPMENT

PATTERN PAPER AND CARD

Dressmaker's squared paper used for enlarging the book patterns can be bought from fabric and craft stores. This is usually supplied with 5cm (2in) squares and to adapt it you will need to draw onto it, in a contrast colour, a 2.5cm (1in) grid. You can make your own square (graph) paper using large sheets of plain paper, a rule marked in centimetres or inches, a 90° set square and a soft pencil to draw out the grid. An eraser is useful and a pen can also be used to remark the grid lines more permanently. Medium thickness card is needed to make long-lasting patterns.

SCISSORS

A pair of good quality sharp scissors with 10cm (4in) blades is best for cutting fabric. Small sharp pointed embroidery scissors are used for snipping or unpicking threads and cutting small parts. The curved blades of manicure scissors will cut features smoothly.

SEWING NEEDLES AND PINS

A selection of hand sewing needles will enable you to choose the one which suits you and the fabric best. Use a strong needle when sewing calico. Long darning needles are useful for sewing through a limb and for working with yarn to make a hair style. Pins with coloured heads or long dressmaker's pins should be used. Count both the number of pins used and also those then removed from the fabric to make sure that none are left in the toy. Always replace unused pins in a box or pin cushion.

SEWING MACHINE

Although not essential, a sewing machine will make sewing quicker and easier. It will also stitch body seams which have a smooth outline when filled. Use a strong needle when stitching calico or thick fabrics. A zig-zag or overlock stitch is useful to neaten seams of garments.

MAKING AIDS

A compass or plates and glasses are required for drawing circles. A soft pencil or vanishing marking pen is used to transfer sewing positions onto

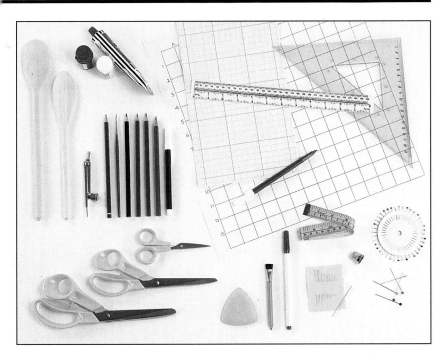

the fabric, or for dark materials a chalk pencil or tailor's chalk will make a visible mark. Dressmaker's carbon paper can be placed between the fabric and pattern or a drawing of the face features, to mark the positions for stitches or embroidery. Eyebrow tweezers are useful to place small glued features. A quick unpicking tool will neatly remove any wrongly placed stitches without risk of snipping the fabric. Use a paper or leather punch to cut out small circles for eyes.

FILLING STICKS

Blunt sticks of various sizes will help to place the filling accurately and firmly where necessary and will help to turn small parts to their right sides out. Wooden spoon handles, a blunt screwdriver, pencil, chopstick, knitting needle (do not use the point) or dowling rod with a smoothly sandpapered end are all suitable.

GLUES

Use a fabric glue which bonds fabric and dries clear. A rubber latex glue is used for paper and card and for sticking yarn to fabric. A quick setting clear glue fixes small items to decorative dolls.

MATERIALS

Before making your doll, decide if it needs to be completely washable or if it is to be a decorative toy and then choose suitable fabrics.

CALICO

Calico is perhaps the most popular material for 'rag' doll making, being strong, closely woven and washable. It can be bought from craft stores and specialist craft mail order suppliers. The four colours available are a creamy natural unbleached, a pale pink, a deep flesh pink and a tan and these are suitable for a wide range of dolls. Calico creases readily and needs to be pressed before making and then again before filling.

STOCKINETTE

Stockinette is a stretch knitted interlock fabric, made in white or flesh pink. It makes a very soft cuddly and attractive dolls' body when filled with a light bouncy fibre, but care must be taken with the filling since the body shape can be over stretched. To avoid this the fabric is often used in a double thickness. The seams can be almost invisible and it is excellent for modelling the features with a needle and thread.

FELT

Because it comes in such a wide range of attractive colours, felt is ideal for toymaking, especially since it does not fray and can be used to cut out small parts. It is a non-woven fabric made from pressed fibres and will not wash well. Most felts are now produced from man-made fibres. Quality can vary widely. If you are using a large piece, hold it up to the light to check if there are any uneven or thin patches which will tear. Felt can be backed with non-woven lightweight stretch interfacing. This is recommended if it is to be used for boots or shoes for the dolls. Courtelle fleece can also be used to make a simple soft bodied doll.

THREADS

A sewing thread with man-made fibres is suitable for all seams and will give a little when body parts are turned to right side out and filled. Choose a strong matching thread to sew limbs to the body and to close the gap after filling. A soft cotton embroidery thread can be used for the hair of small dolls, and a stranded silk embroidery thread which can be divided into one or two strands is best for eyes, nose and mouth.

FILLING

A good quality white polyester filling was used for all the dolls in this book. There are several grades produced; use the best quality that you can obtain. It should be light and springy when crushed. A filling which looks heavy and lumpy in the bag will not make an attractive toy. A white fibre is satisfactory for all toys but a dark filling will show through a light fabric. Polyester and Dacron fillings are washable and non-allergic. Kapok is a natural fibre, it is not washable and is messy to use but has a soft feel. Foam chips are not recommended for children's toys. Only new, clean and flame retardant fillings should be used when making any toys.

INTERFACINGS

There is a wide range of interfacings and bonding materials available which are very useful to the dollmaker. It is easier to embroider features onto a doll's face which is backed with lightweight stretch interfacing. Two layers of felt bonded together will make a firm brim for a hat.

PATTERN PREPARATION

The patterns for the dolls are given in two ways. For simple shapes the measurements only are given in the text. Using a rule draw these shapes to the correct size onto your pattern paper or card, mark with the names and parts and cut them out. The book patterns are printed onto a grid. Each square of the printed grid represents 2.5cm (1in).

To enlarge and make the patterns you need dressmaker's squared paper or plain paper, a rule, a 90° set square, a soft pencil, a fibre-tipped pen, eraser and thin card. Tracing paper and paper clips are optional. To store the patterns, use a large envelope or tape to keep them together.

Dressmaker's paper is printed with thicker lines forming a 5cm (2in) grid over narrower lines. The paper must be subdivided into 2.5cm (1in) squares using a contrast coloured pen to mark the new grid. If preferred you can mark your own grid on plain paper using a pencil, set square and long rule. Take care to keep the measurements accurate and the lines at right angles whichever paper you use. Number the lines across the top of the paper and letter the lines at the side, and mark the book grid to correspond. This will help to identify the pattern line which is being copied. If you wish to enlarge several patterns, keep your drawn grid as a master and fix a sheet of tracing paper firmly over it with paper clips for each pattern. If the tracing paper moves, the enlarged pattern will not be accurate. Carefully plot the printed pattern onto the tracing or enlarged grid marking each line where the pattern crosses it. Note the shape of the printed pattern between the grid lines and copy it onto the larger squares. No special skill is needed but care and precision are important. Mark all sewing details, the doll's name and pattern part onto each piece and cut out the pattern carefully. For permanent patterns, redraw shapes onto card.

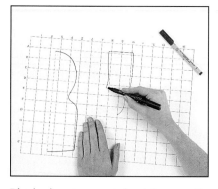

Plot book patterns onto hand-drawn grid and cut out shapes.

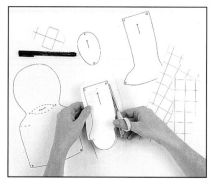

For permanent patterns redraw shapes onto card and cut out.

Where a symetrical shape is needed, only half the pattern may be printed. To make a complete pattern where required, place the enlarged pattern onto a double-sized piece of folded paper with the pattern centre line laid on the fold. Cut around the pattern but not along the fold.

CUTTING OUT

Press all creases from the fabric to be used and lay it out with the right side downwards. Check the 'straight' of the fabric grain. This is shown by the threads which run parallel to the selvedge. If you are using a scrap of fabric without a selvedge, then a single thread, close to the edge, can be pulled to show the grain. The pattern arrows indicate how this 'straight' of grain must lie.

It is helpful to cut extra pattern shapes from scrap paper to make the correct number of each, such as two bodies, four arms, etc. Lay out all the patterns onto the wrong side of the fabric before cutting any out. Take care between cutting two and one pair. Remember to reverse the pattern, once, to make a pair and also to reverse the sewing marks. Lightly draw around the card patterns using a soft pencil, or a chalk pencil on dark fabrics. Do not use a pen or felt tip since this will come off on your fingers when cutting out. Carefully cut around the outline and mark sewing instructions onto the materials.

A fabric strip for binding must be cut on the true bias with the fabric grain on it's diagonal to allow the binding to lie flat when sewn. When cutting fur fabric, the pattern arrows indicate the stroke of the pile. Always take care to cut fur backing fabric only, using the points of small scissors to avoid damaging the pile.

Mark around all patterns reversing one to make a pair if necessary.

Cut out. fabric. Mark sewing positions with a soft pencil or threads.

SEWING TECHNIQUES

Many of the illustrated steps use a contrast thread to demonstrate the sewing technique clearly. When making the doll, use a thread to match the fabric. Unless otherwise stated all seams are made on the wrong sides of two pieces which are matched, pinned and tacked (or basted) before stitching. The seams can be made by hand or machine and a small back stitch is best for handsewing the body pieces.

If using a machine, a small straight stitch is used for calico. For strength on a large doll, make a second line of stitches close to but outside the first line. A longer machine stitch and one seam only is used on stockinette and fleece. Your machine guide will give the stitches suitable for the various clothing fabrics. Trim calico close to the stitching around small dolls and the hands of larger ones. At any point of stress the raw edges can be oversewn by hand to give greater strength. Do not trim fabric close to the seams of stockinette bodies since the fabric

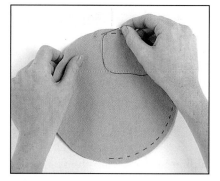

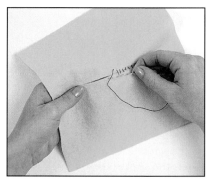

Long running stitches are used to gather fabric, felt and lace.

Ladder stitch is used for closing openings and joining limbs to body.

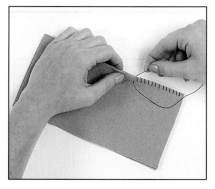

Stab stitches made through fabric and filling make limbs bend and mark fingers.

Oversewing – to attach limbs to body, neaten seams and join fabric.

stitches can 'run'. A long hand running stitch is used to gather fabric. Use a needle and a thread of the length to be gathered. Sew two small back stitches to secure the thread at the beginning then make even straight stitches along the edge to be gathered. Pull up fabric to the required size, make two more back stitches to fasten thread.

A ladder stitch is ideal for closing gaps after filling and for attaching limbs, because it is almost invisible. When closing a gap begin at one end and secure the thread in the seam allowance. Take the needle across the opening and make a running stitch on the right side of the fabric on the seam line parallel to the raw edge, then pass the needle back across the opening to the opposite side and make a similar stitch. Repeat with several more stitches on each side of the opening, then pull the thread and the raw edges will fold into the toy.

Oversewing by hand is used to join the raw edges of two pieces of fabric. It will hold them together before stitching a seam or reinforcing or neatening it. Oversewing is sometimes the only stitch needed for felts. To make the stitch, with raw edges even push the needle and thread through the fabrics from back to front. Take the needle and thread over the edge of the fabrics and insert the needle again 6mm (¼in) from the first stitch. Keep the stitches even and level. A matching zig-zag stitch can often be used to replace oversewing.

FILLING AND FINISHING

When the seams are stitched, check that all are secure. Clip the seam allowance to the stitches around curves and trim around hands and small parts made of calico before turning. Ease out the limbs with the filling stick and smooth all seams between fore finger and thumb.

Some dolls need to be soft and pliable while others should be firm. The head, neck and shoulders are well filled to prevent the head wobbling. When filling limbs place small pieces of fibre in the hands and feet and gradually build up the limb with larger pieces. Try clothes on filled body before they are finally stitched.

HAIR STYLES

Yarn, fur fabric and artifical doll's hair have been used in the book. Yarn is washable and can be styled in many ways. Embroidered eyes should tone with the hair colour. Yarn hair must be sewn firmly in place and can also be glued to the head. Fur fabric of a medium-length pile will make excellent hair for a boy or baby doll. The pile should brush towards the face and the fabric is sewn to the head.

Artificial hair is not washable and will shed individual strands, but it is realistic. Do not use on a small child's toy.

FACIAL FEATURES

A calico doll can have the features embroidered before making. The satin stitch used for the embroidery consists of short straight stitches worked so close together that they touch. A simple mouth is formed by a straight stitch or one that is caught in the centre by a small single stitch to form a curve. Fabric paints or permanent marker pens also make excellent features – they are easy to use and are washable. Draw the front head onto an oversize piece of fabric since it will be easier to

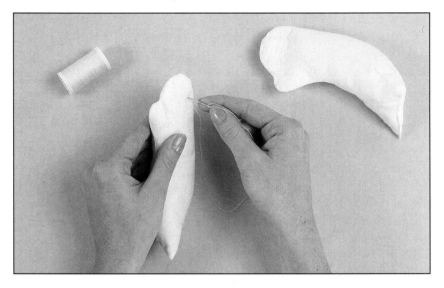

After making the arms, the fingers and thumb can be modelled with stitches. Take the needle and thread vertically through the arm to make small stab stitches. Pull the thread to mould the fabric and filling.

handle while working the features and can be cut to the pattern shape later when you are satisfied. It is a good idea to practice on paper or fabric with several faces before marking the position onto the doll with a soft pencil. Felt features are sewn in place after the toy is finished. Small circles for eyes can be cut with a paper or leather punch.

For added expression, a few modelling stitches can be used. You need a long needle and double matching sewing thread. For these, fasten the thread end at the centre back of the head, take the needle through the head to the inner corner of the eye, then take a second stitch very close to the first one beside the eye and back through the head. Pull the thread and see if you like the way the face is dented then fasten the thread.

SAFETY

Toys made for sale must conform to safety standards and most countries have their own code. However, the doll maker has an equal responsibility for toys made as gifts. For young children the doll should be suitable for the child's age, with all small parts sewn firmly in place. Filling and fabrics where possible should be flame-proof and any paints, pens, crayons or glues that are used must be non-toxic.

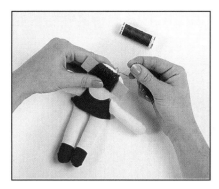

Making Hair Styles

To make fringe for either a boy or girl doll, wind yarn around a piece of card to form loops. Place card to centre front of head and sew each loop to head seam. Remove card and sew across loops to hold them close to front head.

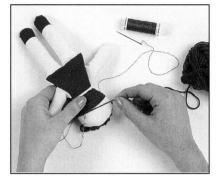

The back hair, for a doll with plaits, can be made by covering the head with a continous length of yarn. Thread two needles and sew end of yarn to head side seam on lower hair line. Take yarn across back head to corresponding point on opposite head seam and sew to the head with the second needle. Continue until whole head is covered.

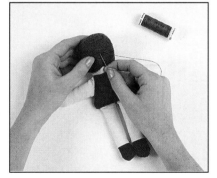

To complete the back hair, with matching thread sew yarn strands to back head along a centre parting.

For front hair of a boy or girl doll, cut strands of yarn of required number and length. Place yarn onto head to cover join of fringe and back hair. Sew each strand to head along a centre parting from front to back of head. Sew each group of strands to front head on seam at lower edge of back hair. Plait hair and tie with ribbon.

A boy doll has back hair made by winding yarn around a larger piece of card. The yarn loops are sewn around back head, the card removed and the loops are flattened and sewn to back head just above hair line to keep them close to head. The gap between back hair and fringe is covered by front hair sewn to head on a centre parting and side seams. Trim yarn to a boy's hair style.

MATERIALS: *Small amount of each fabric – pink calico, blue felt, check fabric, red fabric; lightweight interfacing; scrap of black felt; brown double knitting yarn; narrow elastic and bodkin; matching sewing threads; scrap of red embroidery thread; red crayon; filling; thin card*

Cut out all pieces. Press interfacing to one cap peak before cutting out. Cut two straps from check fabric 4cm × 12cm (1½in × 4¾in). Seam allowance is ½cm (⅜in) – this also applies to Teresa Twin. Stitch a head to a body at neck A–A. Repeat for second pair.

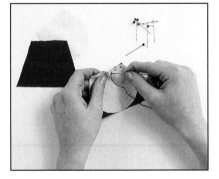

Stitch foot to leg B–D–B. Fold leg and foot along centre line C–D–E. Lightly mark foot curve onto fabric. Stitch leg seam F–B and around curve of foot B–E. Trim fabric close to seam. Turn leg through to right side and press. Fill lightly with stuffing and oversew open edges to enclose stuffing. Make second leg.

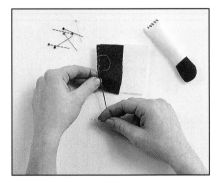

Place raw edges of legs to right side of one of the body pieces F–C. Baste then stitch legs to body. Fold an arm along centre line A–G. Lightly mark curve of hand onto fabric. Stitch seam H–K leaving open A–H. Trim fabric close to seam. Turn arm to right side out and press. Lightly fill with stuffing and oversew open edges.

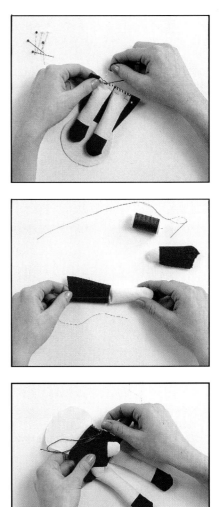

Stitch a narrow hem at sleeve wrist J–J. Stitch sleeve seam H–J. Turn sleeve to right side out and press. Sew a line of running stitches along upper edge between dots to gather the edge. Fit sleeve onto arm, pull up gathers to fit and oversew raw edges of sleeve to raw edges of arm. Make second arm and sleeve.

Place arms onto right side of body with raw edges even, matching A–H. **Note:** The arms will cross the body in centre front while this is done and when body side seams are stitched. Baste raw edges of arms and body together.

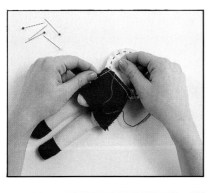

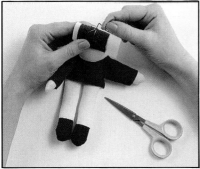

With right sides together stitch bodies together at side seams, including arms and around head L–H–A–A–H–L but leaving open lower straight edges. Turn body through to right side and press. Fill with stuffing. Turn ends of legs to inside of body, turn under opposite raw edge and sew across lower straight edge L–L to cover top of legs and enclose body stuffing.

For the fringe, cut a piece of card 7cm × 3cm (2¾in × 1¼in). Wind 20 strands of brown knitting yarn around shorter width. Hold one long edge of card to centre front of head seam with yarn to front of head and oversew fold of each strand to fabric. Slide card from loops and sew strands to head in front of seam line to hold flat.

For back hair, cut card 10cm × 6cm (4in × 2½in). Wind yarn around shorter width until card is covered, push strands together until they fit head covering head seam to above ear positions. Sew upper fold of each strand to head seam. Remove card.

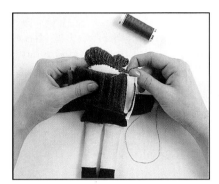

Cut 30 strands of yarn each 20cm (8in) long. Hold all strands together at their centre and sew to head at a centre parting with yarn covering join of fringe and back hair. Smooth hair over head and sew strands to cover side seams and across back head at natural hair line. Cut loops and trim yarn.

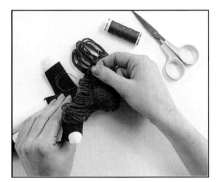

Cut two small black felt circles (paper punch size) for eyes. Take a stitch through head from back to front and through eye, then through eye again and head. Pull thread and secure. For mouth embroider two small straight stitches into a V shape using two strands of red embroidery thread. With same thread make a tiny stitch for nose. Mark cheeks and eyebrows with red crayon.

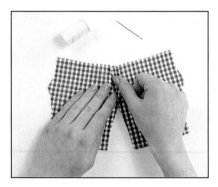

Stitch trouser pieces together at one centre (front) seam only M–N and press open. Stitch narrow hems at legs P–P.

Fold and stitch a double hem at waist to form casing for elastic. Thread through elastic sewing it at one end to fabric. Pull up to fit waist and sew other end to secure. Trim excess elastic. Stitch remaining centre seam M–N. Stitch inner leg seams P–N–P. Turn trousers to right side out and fit onto doll. With wrong sides facing, fold and press straps along length in centre.

Turn in raw edges of straps to meet centre fold and top stitch together. Top stitch opposite edge. Place straps across doll's shoulders crossing them at back. Tuck strap ends inside trousers and sew to waist gathers. Cut two small circles of blue felt as buttons (use a shirt button as a template) and sew to ends of straps at front.

Press to wrong side a single hem 1cm ($\frac{3}{8}$in) around edge of cap Q–T–Q. Press a further 1cm ($\frac{3}{8}$in) single hem to wrong side around edge. Pleat or gather second fold to lie flat. Stitch very close to folded edge and to outer edge to form a channel. Thread through elastic and sew one end to fabric. Gather fabric to 18cm (7in), secure and trim excess elastic.

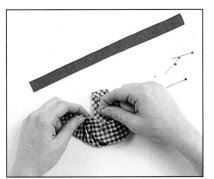

Stitch curved edges of peaks together R–S–S–R. Trim fabric close to stitches. Turn peak to right side out and press. Baste open edges together. With right sides facing stitch peak to gathered cap matching T's. By hand oversew raw edges of peak and cap together. Stitch cap seam Q–W–Q. Cut blue felt scarf 25cm × 1.5cm (10in × $\frac{5}{8}$in). Cut a fringe at short ends.

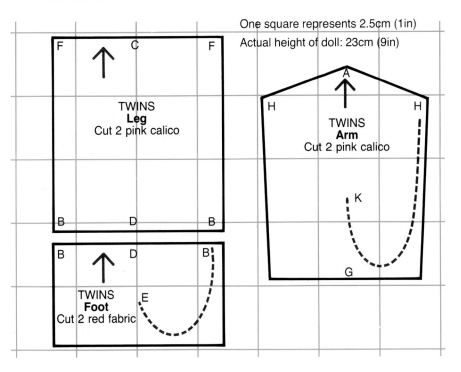

One square represents 2.5cm (1in)
Actual height of doll: 23cm (9in)

TWINS
Leg
Cut 2 pink calico

TWINS
Foot
Cut 2 red fabric

TWINS
Arm
Cut 2 pink calico

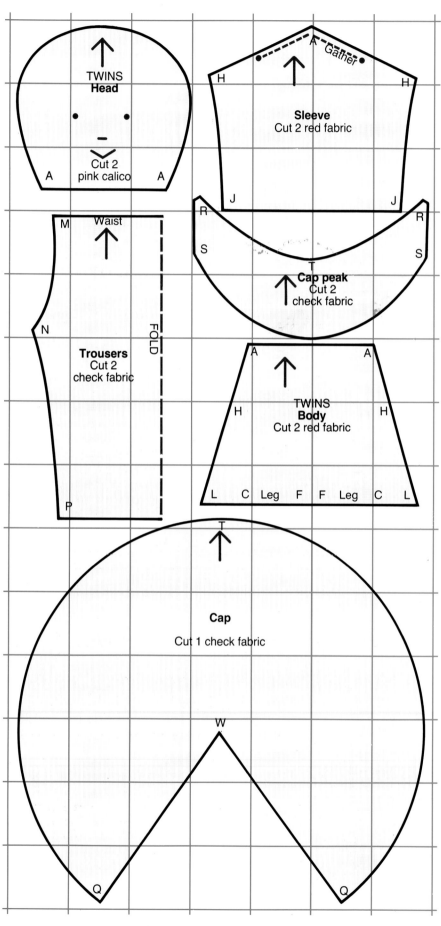

TWINS
Head

Cut 2
pink calico

A   A

Sleeve
Cut 2 red fabric

H   H

Gather

J   J

R   R

S   S

T
Cap peak
Cut 2
check fabric

M   Waist

N

FOLD

Trousers
Cut 2
check fabric

P

A   A

H   **TWINS**
Body
Cut 2 red fabric   H

L C Leg F   F Leg C L

T

Cap

Cut 1 check fabric

W

Q   Q

MATERIALS: *Small amounts of each fabric—pink calico; red fabric; spotted fabric; 130cm (51in) narrow lace; 1m (1yd) very narrow satin ribbon; scrap of black felt; brown double knitting yarn; narrow elastic and bodkin; scrap of stranded red embroidery thread; red crayon; filling; thin card*

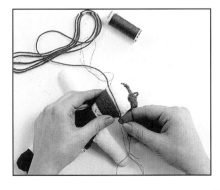

Cut out skirt 10cm × 42cm (4in x 16½in) and two straps 4cm × 10cm (1½in × 4in). Follow steps 1–6 of Tom Twin. Sew lace around neck and lower edge of body. Follow Tom Twin step 7; loops remain uncut. For back hair, secure yarn 1cm (⅜in) above neck seam just in front of side seam with one needle. Take yarn across back of head and secure with second needle.

Continue to take strands of yarn across back of head keeping them very close together and sewing at each seam with separate needle and thread. Cover whole back head to top seam. Sew the centre back of hair to head to form a parting, pulling up lower strands to make a natural hair line.

For the plaits cut 21 strands of yarn each 43cm (17in) long. Sew centre of each strand to centre of head from front to back for 1cm (⅜in) each side of head seam to cover fringe stitches. Gather each bunch of hair to front of face and sew at lower edge of back hair. Plait hair and tie with red thread. Trim plaits.

Follow step 8–10 of Tom Twin. Stitch a narrow hem at one long edge of skirt. Stitch lace to wrong side to show below. Stitch ribbon to right side above hem. Stitch a double hem at opposite long edge to form a casing. Thread through elastic using bodkin and sew at one end to fabric. Pull up to fit waist, sew to fabric and trim elastic. Stitch short edges of skirt together.

Press under a single hem to wrong side of curved edge of a shoulder frill X–X. Stitch lace to wrong side over hem edge, to show beyond fabric. Sew a line of long running stitches along straight edge, pull up stitches to gather frill to 4cm (1½in) and secure thread. Make second frill.

With wrong sides facing fold and press a strap piece along centre length. Turn in raw edges to centre fold and press. Insert and baste gathered edge of a frill into a folded strap at centre of length. Top stitch together open edges of strap with frill in-between. Make second strap and frill. Place straps on doll, crossing them at back. Tuck ends into skirt waist and sew.

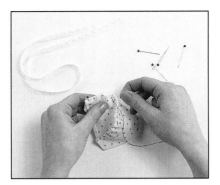

Stitch curved edge of bonnet brims Y–V–V–Y together leaving open straight edges Y–Z–Y. Trim fabric close to stitches and turn brim to right side out. Press and baste open edges together. Turn under and stitch a narrow hem at straight edge of bonnet back Y–Y. Stitch brim to bonnet back Y–Z–Y. Stitch lace inside of brim and lower edge of back. Sew ribbons to sides at Y.

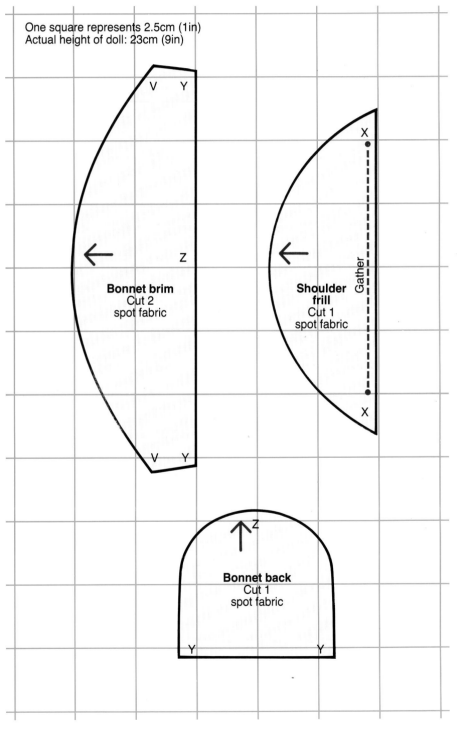

One square represents 2.5cm (1in)
Actual height of doll: 23cm (9in)

Bonnet brim
Cut 2
spot fabric

Shoulder frill
Cut 1
spot fabric

Gather

Bonnet back
Cut 1
spot fabric

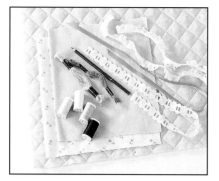

MATERIALS: 36cm × 40cm (14in × 16in) quilted fabric; 20cm × 20cm (8in × 8in) pink fabric; 15cm × 20cm (6in × 8in) printed fabric; 110cm × 2cm (43in × 3/4in) pre-gathered broderie anglaise edging; 13cm × 2cm (5in × 3/4in) wide slotted broderie anglaise trimming; 60cm × 1cm (24in × 3/8in) wide satin ribbon; yellow soft embroidery thread; pink stranded embroidery thread; black stranded embroidery thread; matching sewing threads; pink crayon; filling

A simple-to-make doll for a small child. The doll could also be filled with pot-pourri as an adult sleep pillow. The doll's size could be enlarged to make a hot water bottle cover. The doll is made on one side of the body only and is completed before the body pieces are stitched together.

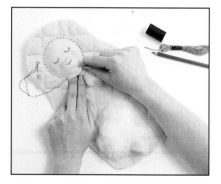

Cut out all pieces. Draw features lightly onto the pink face. Using two strands of pink thread embroider eyelids and mouth in chain stitch and nose with tiny straight stitches. Embroider eye-lashes with single black stitches. Mark cheeks with pink crayon. Baste the face edge to one body piece leaving open between A–B. Add filling to face through opening.

Wind yellow embroidery thread 12 times around a pencil to form loops. Leave loops on pencil and with a needle and thread sew loops to each other in a straight line. Slip the loops off the pencil, trim ends of thread and sew loops in a line to centre top of face.

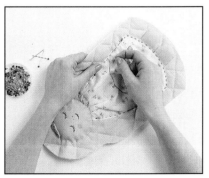

Slot ribbon through broiderie anglaise trimming and stitch to right side of dress. Trim ends. Sew long running stitches across dress A–B. Pull up gathers to fit face A–B and secure thread. Slip gathered edge of dress under face. Baste face through dress and body A–B. Pin dress to body, leaving slightly full. Place feet between dress and body at lower edge C–D and baste dress to body.

Stitch hands and feet together in pairs leaving open straight edges C–D. Trim fabric close to seams, turn to right side out and press. Fill lightly and oversew raw edges to enclose stuffing. Cut 8cm (3in) broiderie anglaise edging. With raw edges of hand and straight edge of trimming even, baste edging around hands with edging ends at centre of one side. The feet are not trimmed.

With raw edges even baste hands to right side of dress C–D. Cut 16cm (6in) broiderie anglaise edging, turn under ends and stitch to lower edge of dress across feet with the straight edge covering previous basting stitches. Baste a second piece of edging around dress including hands and feet.

Stitch edging around face with ends at centre neck. With right sides together stitch the two body pieces together, leaving open one side between dots. Turn body through to right side. Fill lightly with stuffing, turn in open edges and sew together. Tie a ribbon bow and sew to centre neck.

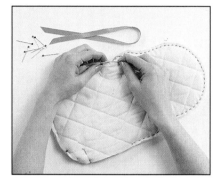

One square represents 2.5cm (1in)

Actual height of doll: 32cm (12½in)

A — Gather — B

↑

C — C

Dress
Cut 1 print fabric

D — D

Trimming placement

C — D C — D

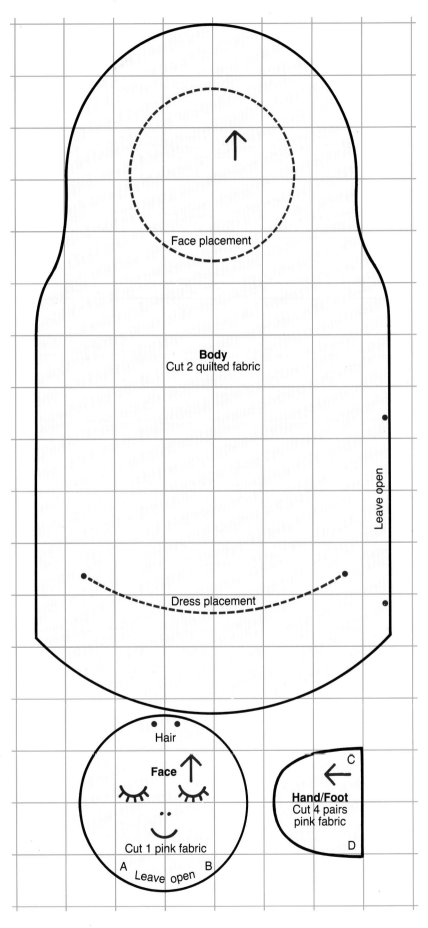

Face placement

Body
Cut 2 quilted fabric

Leave open

Dress placement

Hair

Face

Cut 1 pink fabric

A   Leave open   B

C

Hand/Foot
Cut 4 pairs
pink fabric

D

MATERIALS: *40cm × 80cm (16in × 31 in) pink calico; 20cm × 80cm (8in × 31in) red and white gingham fabric; 26cm × 42cm (10in × 17in) blue denim fabric; 20cm × 60cm (8in × 24in) fawn felt; 12cm × 32cm (5in × 13in) dark brown felt; 16cm × 40cm (6in × 16in) red felt; scrap of blue felt; 8cm × 25cm (3in × 10in) golden brown fur fabric (pile to stroke down shorter length); three small press fasteners; narrow elastic; bonding web; filling; matching and orange sewing threads; red crayon; red embroidery thread; 1m (1yd) piping cord*

TEX, THE COWBOY

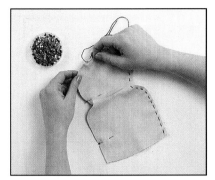

Cut out all parts. See step 12 before cutting hat brim. Stitch dart at neck on both bodies A–A. With right sides together stitch bodies leaving open lower edge B–B. Turn body through to right side and press. Fill head and neck firmly with stuffing, moulding to a good even shape. Fill body more softly. Turn under lower edges and sew together to enclose filling.

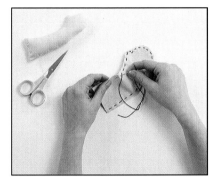

Stitch arms together in pairs leaving open C–D. Trim seam and snip fabric to dot at thumb, turn arm through to the right side and press. Fill softly with stuffing, turn in open edges and sew together.

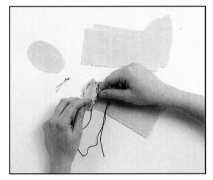

Stitch legs E–F and G–H and trim seams at foot. Baste foot soles to legs F–H and stitch in place. Turn legs to right side out and press. Fill feet firmly and the legs more softly with stuffing. Turn in raw edges and sew together.

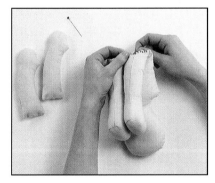

With feet facing forward pin straight edges of legs to lower edge of body and oversew in place.

Position and pin straight edges of arms onto shoulders with thumbs upwards and oversew firmly to body.

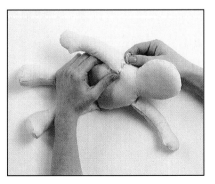

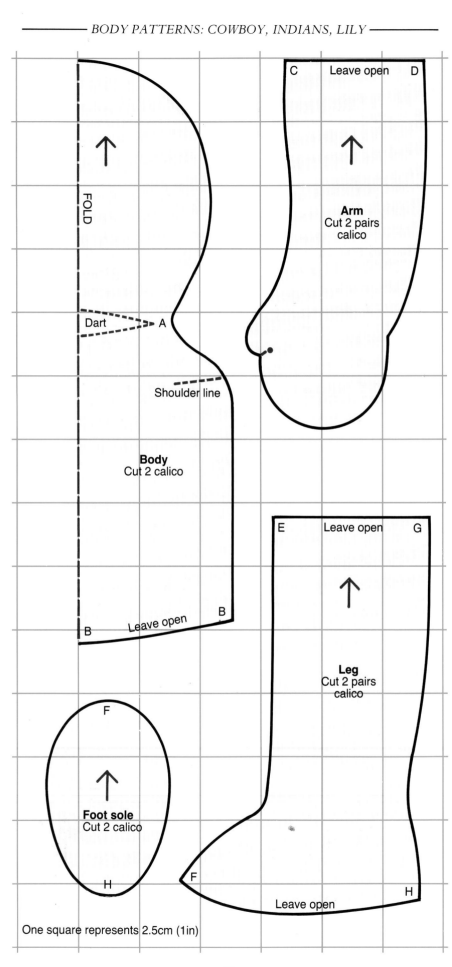

FOLD

Dart → A

Shoulder line

Body
Cut 2 calico

C   Leave open   D

↑

Arm
Cut 2 pairs
calico

B   Leave open   B

E   Leave open   G

↑

Leg
Cut 2 pairs
calico

F

↑

Foot sole
Cut 2 calico

H   F

H

Leave open

One square represents 2.5cm (1in)

To make hair, with right sides facing oversew the two shorter edges together. Stroke fur towards one long edge, turn under this edge and slip stitch to wrong side. Sew running stitches along opposite edge to gather it. Pull up stitches as tightly as possible and secure thread. Turn hair to right side out and pull onto head bringing to a low hair line in front. Sew to head.

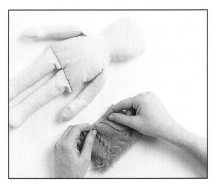

Lightly mark position for features onto face. From brown felt cut two circles for eyes and sew in place. Mark nose with red crayon. Embroider mouth with three straight red stitches.

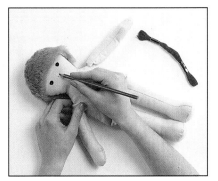

Stitch shirt sleeves to shirt front and to shirt backs J–K. Turn under and stitch a narrow double hem at sleeve wrist edges L–L and at centre front edges M–N. Stitch underarm seams L–K and shirt fronts to back at side seams K–P. Stitch a double hem at lower edge N–P–P–N. Turn under neck edge M–J–J–M and stitch. Sew press fasteners to close centre fronts. Fit shirt onto doll.

With orange thread stitch two lines of machine stitches 6mm (¼in) apart on side fold of each jeans' piece. For pockets cut two pieces of denim 5cm x 5cm (2in × 2in). Press under edges and top stitch one edge in orange. With matching thread stitch centre front seam Q–R on one side only. Lay jeans right side upwards, position pockets and stitch three edges. Stitch felt patch to one knee.

Turn to wrong side a narrow double hem at lower legs S–S and stitch. Turn down and stitch a double hem at waist to form a casing. Thread through elastic and stitch it firmly at one end. Pull up elastic to fit doll's waist and stitch elastic to secure it.

Stitch remaining seam Q–R and inside leg seams S–R–S. Fit jeans onto doll turning up lower legs.

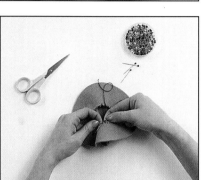

Cut an oversize piece of felt for hat brim and bond to a second piece following manufacturer's instructions. Cut out one brim from bonded felt. Stitch hat crowns together leaving open lower edges T–T. Turn crown to right side out, insert it into brim T–T and oversew it on underside of brim. Press brim.

Cut a strip of dark brown felt 1.5cm x 23cm (⅝in × 9in) and sew around outside of crown as a hat band. Add filling to hat crown and place hat onto head with crown seams to sides and the crown covering centre of hair. Sew hat to head.

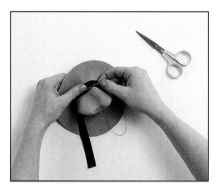

Stitch front seam of boots W–F. Turn seam to inside. With wrong sides facing baste boot sole to boot F–H–F and top stitch. Fit boots onto cowboy. Cut the scarf from blue felt and tie around the neck.

Stitch waistcoat fronts to back at shoulders V–X. Press seams. Machine a row of stitches just inside armhole edges Y–X–Y, through single felt. Stitch side seams Y–Z. Make a line of machine stitches just inside edges of fronts and back. Fold one end of cord into a small loop to fit hand, the other into a larger loop. Bind ends of cord with thread to secure. Sew lasso to hands.

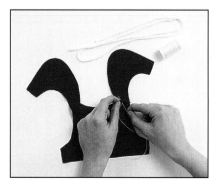

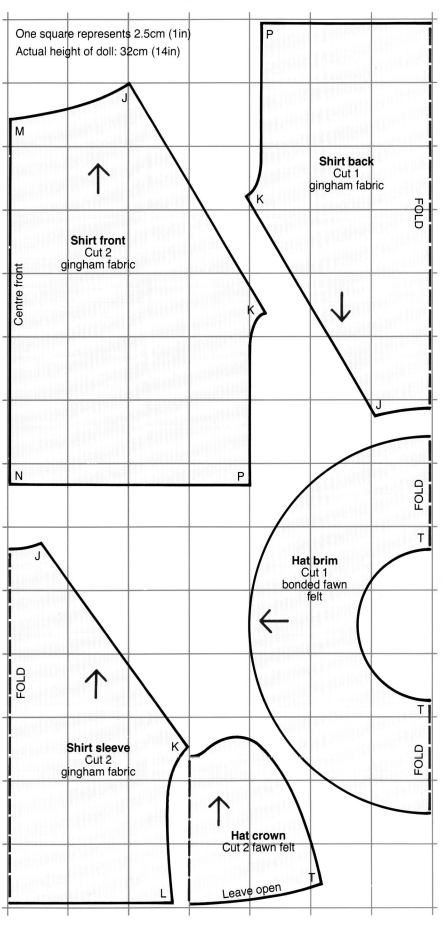

One square represents 2.5cm (1in)
Actual height of doll: 32cm (14in)

Shirt back
Cut 1
gingham fabric

Shirt front
Cut 2
gingham fabric

Hat brim
Cut 1
bonded fawn
felt

Shirt sleeve
Cut 2
gingham fabric

Hat crown
Cut 2 fawn felt

Leave open

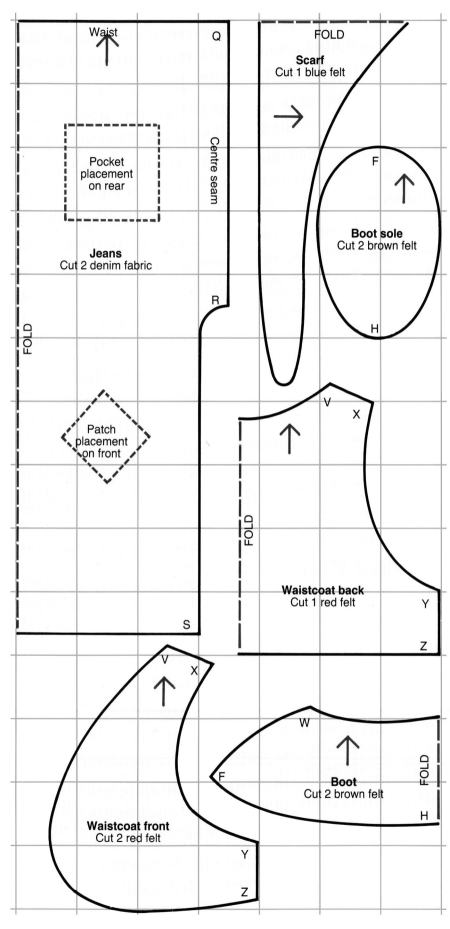

Waist

Q

FOLD

Scarf
Cut 1 blue felt

Centre seam

Pocket
placement
on rear

F

Jeans
Cut 2 denim fabric

Boot sole
Cut 2 brown felt

R

H

FOLD

Patch
placement
on front

V

X

FOLD

Waistcoat back
Cut 1 red felt

Y

S

Z

V

X

W

F

Boot
Cut 2 brown felt

FOLD

H

Waistcoat front
Cut 2 red felt

Y

Z

MATERIALS: 40cm × 80cm (16in × 31in) brown calico: 61cm × 61cm (24in × 24in) fawn felt; 14cm × 24cm (5½in × 9in) yellow felt; scrap of black felt; 140cm (55in) decorative braid; black double knitting yarn; 6cm (2¼in) narrow black tape; narrow elastic and bodkin; 3 small press fasteners; matching sewing threads; red braid for neck band; red embroidery thread; 3 feathers; black crayon

Follow steps 1–5 of Cowboy to make body. For back hair, thread two needles with black sewing threads. With first needle secure end of yarn to just in front of head side seam 1.5cm (⅝in) above back neck seam. Take yarn across back head to opposite seam and sew with second needle. Cover back head to top seam. Sew parting down centre back pulling up lower strands.

For front hair cut 40 strands of yarn 55cm (22in) long. Turn under ends of black tape and sew centre of each strand to centre of tape. Lightly mark centre front of head on forehead 2.5cm (1in) below seam. Sew tape to head with one end at front centre mark and the other end covering back hair. Bring hair to front of doll and sew to head over seam at lower edge of back hair.

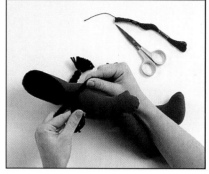

Plait hair and tie ends with red thread. Trim ends of hair. Lightly mark position for features onto face. Cut two black felt circles for eyes, sew a white thread highlight in centre of each and sew to head. Embroider mouth with two straight red stitches. Mark eyebrows, nose and inner corners of eyes with pen.

With right sides facing match trouser pieces together in pairs. Place **uncut** felt fringe, with one long edge even with trouser side edges, between dots. Stitch seam J–K including fringe. Stitch second fringe and side seam. Stitch trouser pieces together at centre front seam only M–N. Press seam open and side seams towards back. Stitch both edges of braid to right side of ankles L–K–L.

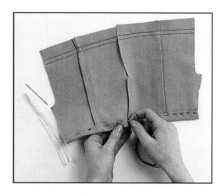

Turn under and stitch single hem at waist to form a casing. Thread through elastic until one end is level with felt and stitch through elastic and casing to secure. Pull up elastic to fit doll, stitch other end of elastic to secure and trim excess. Stitch centre back seam M–N and inside leg seams L–N–L. Turn trousers to right side out and snip leg and side fringes.

Stitch jacket sleeves to jacket back P–Q. Stitch sleeves to fronts P–Q. Press seams open. On right side stitch braid to sleeves R–R. Stitch fronts to back at side seams Q–S and underarm seams Q–R. On right side stitch braid to lower edges of jacket. Fold under and stitch a single hem at centre fronts X–W.

Stitch collar to wrong side of jacket neck matching dots at centre back and at X's in the front. Turn collar over raw edges to right side out. Cut fringes at collar, wrists and lower edges of jacket. Fit jacket onto doll, overlap fronts and sew a press fastener at the neck, centre and lower edges, to close them.

Cut a braid band to fit around head and oversew ends. Cut feathers, if too long, and tuck them into band at back and sew feathers and band to head.

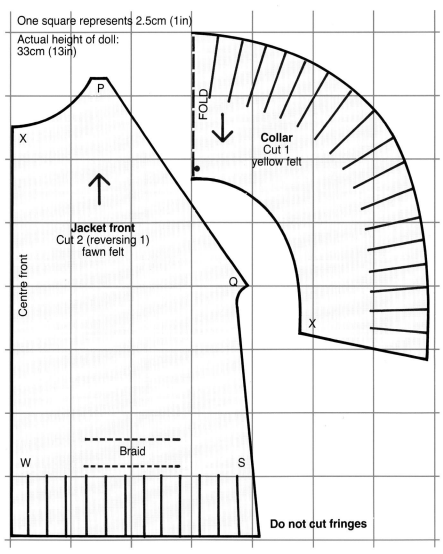

One square represents 2.5cm (1in)

Actual height of doll: 33cm (13in)

P

X

FOLD

Collar
Cut 1
yellow felt

Jacket front
Cut 2 (reversing 1)
fawn felt

Centre front

Q

X

Braid

W

S

Do not cut fringes

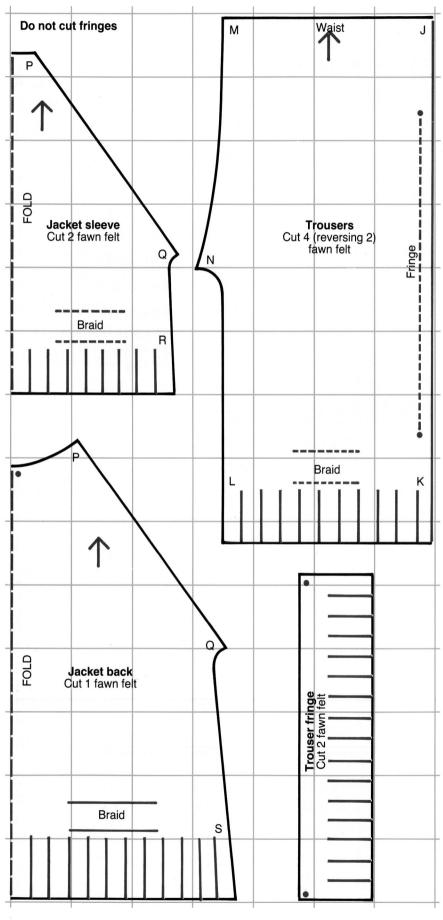

Do not cut fringes

P

FOLD

Jacket sleeve
Cut 2 fawn felt

Q

N

M

Waist

J

Fringe

Trousers
Cut 4 (reversing 2)
fawn felt

Braid

R

P

FOLD

Jacket back
Cut 1 fawn felt

Q

Braid

S

L

Braid

K

Trouser fringe
Cut 2 fawn felt

MATERIALS: *40cm × 80cm (16in × 13in) brown calico; 26cm × 90cm (10in × 36in) orange felt; scrap of black felt; 110cm (43in) decorative braid; black double knitting wool; matching sewing threads; red embroidery thread; narrow elastic and bodkin; two small press fasteners; one feather; beads (optional)*

Follow steps 1–5 of Cowboy instructions to make body. Follow steps 1–3 of Little Bear's instructions to make hair and face. Do not plait hair but sew it in front of head side seams.

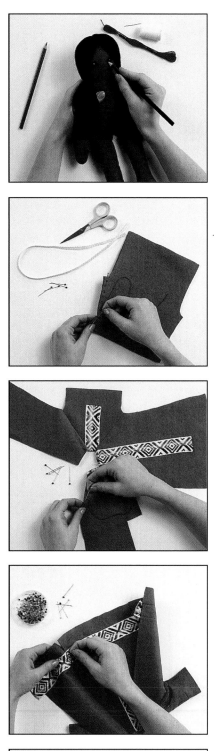

Stitch trouser pieces together at centre front seam only M–N. Turn under and stitch a single hem at waist to form a casing. Thread through elastic until one end is level with felt and stitch through elastic and casing to secure. Pull up elastic to fit doll, stitch other end of elastic through casing and trim excess. Stitch centre back seam M–N. Stitch inside leg seams L–N–L.

Stitch decorative braid to centre front of dress R–W. Stitch braid to centre of sleeves turning under lower ends to neaten. Stitch sleeves to dress front P–Q and to backs P–Q.

Stitch fronts to the back at side seams Q–S and the underarm seams Q–Y. On right side stitch braid to lower edges of dress just above the ends of the side seams W–S–S–W, covering the end of centre front braid.

With right sides together stitch centre backs together X–W. Stitch narrow hems to wrong side T–X. Turn under and stitch a narrow hem at neck. On right side place collar around neck, fold one long edge to inside and hand stitch over hem. Sew press fasteners to close centre back. Cut fringes. Thread beads and sew around neck. See page 39 for head band and feather details.

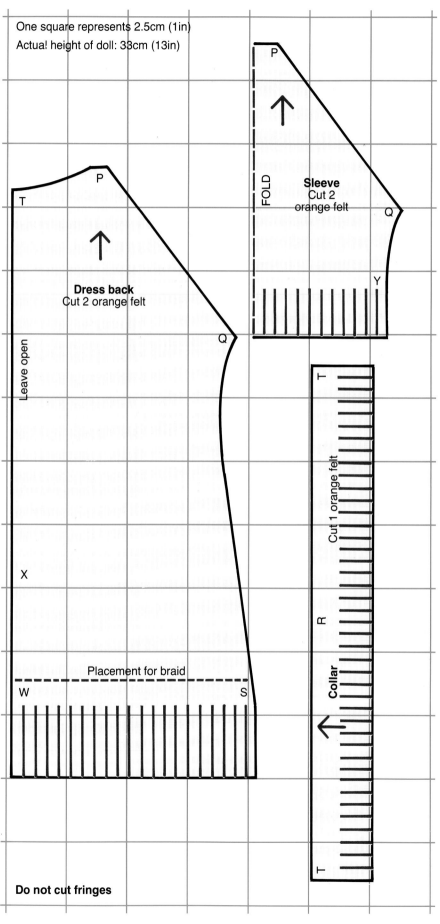

One square represents 2.5cm (1in)

Actual height of doll: 33cm (13in)

P

FOLD

Sleeve
Cut 2
orange felt

Q

Y

T

P

Dress back
Cut 2 orange felt

Q

Leave open

T

Cut 1 orange felt

R

Collar

X

Placement for braid

W

S

Do not cut fringes

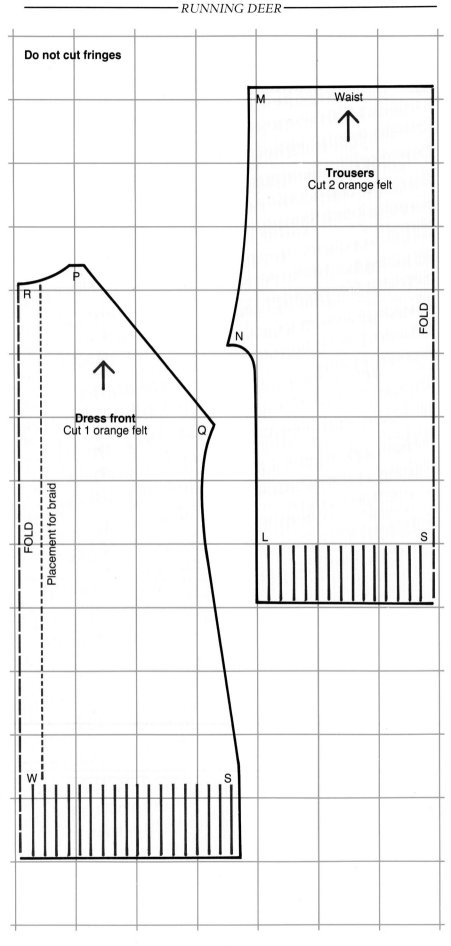

Do not cut fringes

M   Waist

Trousers
Cut 2 orange felt

P

R

FOLD

N

FOLD

Dress front
Cut 1 orange felt

Q

Placement for braid

L   S

W   S

MATERIALS: 40cm × 80cm (16in × 31 in) cream calico; printed fabric and matching bias binding; green felt; scrap of black felt; 120cm (47in) narrow straight decorative binding; 80cm (31½in) ric-rac (or novelty) braid; 20cm (8in) dolls' black mohair; matching sewing threads; narrow elastic and bodkin; three small press fasteners; thin card; black and red crayon; filling; craft glue

Follow steps 1–5 of Cowboy instructions to make body using cream calico. Spread mohair into a single layer to form a fringe and to cover head. Spread glue onto head and allow to dry slightly. Place hair onto head with one end making a low fringe. Pull hair over head seams at sides. When the glue is dry sew hair to head. Trim hair to a fringe and at shoulders.

Lightly mark position for features on face. Cut two black felt eyes, sew a small white thread highlight on each eye and glue eyes to face. Embroider mouth with two straight red stitches. Mark eyebrows with black crayon and nose and cheeks with red crayon.

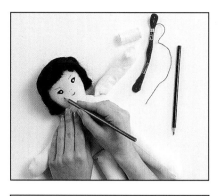

With right sides facing match both trouser pieces. Stitch one centre seam only J–K. Turn under and stitch a narrow double hem at lower edge of legs L–L. Stitch braid over leg hem stitches. Turn under a double hem at waist. Thread elastic through casing, stitching at one end. Pull up to fit waist and secure. Stitch second centre seam J–K and inside leg seams L–K–L.

Stitch a narrow double hem at sleeve wrist edge P–P. Stitch braid over hem stitches. Stitch sleeves to jacket fronts and to jacket back M–N. Open out bias binding and place right side to wrong side of jacket front, with raw edges even. Stitch binding along its fold line to jacket fronts and back Q–M–M–Q. Turn binding over raw edges to right side. Top stitch close to binding edge.

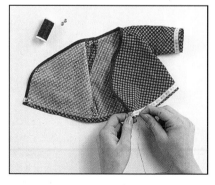

Stitch fronts to back at side seams N–R and underarm seams N–P. Turn under and stitch a narrow double hem at lower edge of jacket Q–R–R–Q. Cut braid slightly longer than this lower edge, turn under ends and on right side stitch braid over seam stitches. Fit jacket onto doll overlapping the fronts. Sew press fasteners in given positions.

Fold upper edge of shoe to wrong side, and stitch a narrow single hem S–T–S. Fold shoes T–V and stitch front seam S–X. Stitch shoe sole to shoe matching X and V. Turn shoe to right side out and fit onto doll. Make second shoe.

From card cut one hat shape. Spread glue on one side of card and press to an oversize piece of felt. Make sure that felt is smooth and note chin strap placement positions. Trim felt to edge of card. Glue felt to second face of card and trim to size. Glue or sew ric-rac braid around upper edge of hat.

Cut 28cm (11in) of ric-rac for chin strap and sew to underside of hat on placement marks. Match edges Y–Y and oversew seam X–Y. Turn hat to right side out, with seam ridge on underside. Press if necessary and fit onto doll. The hat can be sewn to head. **Note:** If making this doll for a small child, use black knitting yarn to make hair (mohair is not washable).

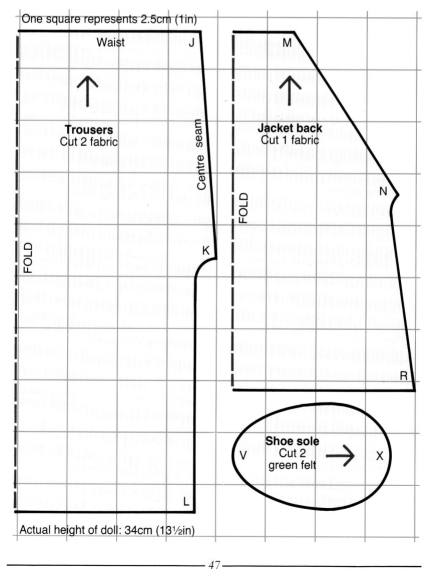

One square represents 2.5cm (1in)

Waist   J

Trousers
Cut 2 fabric

Centre seam

FOLD

K

M

Jacket back
Cut 1 fabric

FOLD

N

R

Shoe sole
Cut 2
green felt

V   X

L

Actual height of doll: 34cm (13½in)

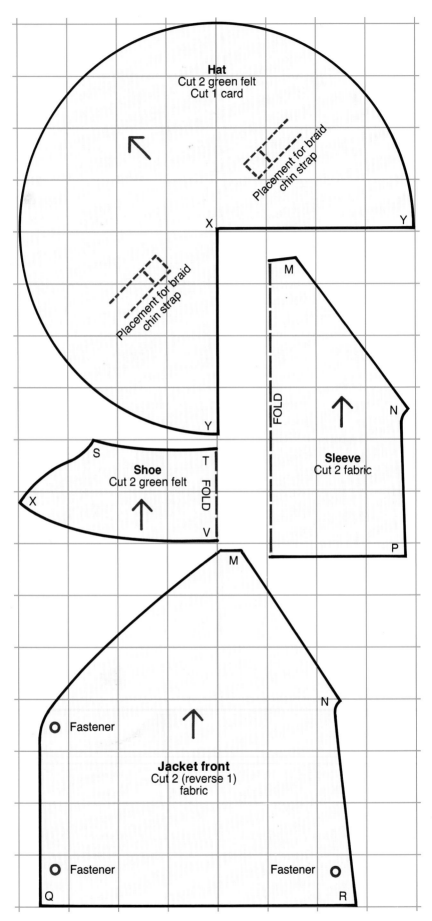

Hat
Cut 2 green felt
Cut 1 card

Placement for braid
chin strap

Placement for braid
chin strap

Sleeve
Cut 2 fabric

Shoe
Cut 2 green felt

FOLD

FOLD

Jacket front
Cut 2 (reverse 1)
fabric

O Fastener

O Fastener

Fastener O

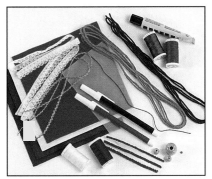

MATERIALS: For one doll – 3 × 10cm (4in) lengths of pipe cleaners, red if possible; 20mm (¾in) diameter polished wooden bead; 2 × 10mm (⅜in) diameter polished wooden beads; red, green, white and brown felts; matching sewing threads; 25cm (10in) red soft embroidery thread; narrow gold ric-rac braid; narrow lace edging (girl); brown knitting yarn; tiny bead for brooch (girl); soft filling; strong clear adhesive; red and black, fine-tip, permanent marker pens; tracing paper

Trace actual size patterns. To make body and head for either doll, squeeze glue into hole of the 20mm (¾in) bead. Hold two pipe cleaners side by side with ends even and push one end of pair halfway into bead. Glue feet together in pairs with opposite ends of a pipe cleaner between each pair – the curved edges of feet make toes of doll.

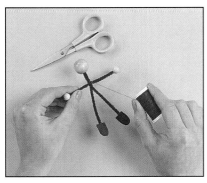

Glue 10mm (⅜in) bead to each end of remaining pipe cleaner for arms. Place arms across body 1.5cm (⅝in) below head and twist them once, tightly around the body. Bind joint of arms and body with red sewing thread. **Note:** Allow glue to dry at each stage of making doll. Use small stitches to oversew seams, by hand, on wrong side.

For both dolls: Sew short edges of hat together, turn seam to inside. Fold red embroidery thread in half and knot ends together. Sew long running stitches around one edge of hat. Pull up stitches to gather, insert thread knot into centre of hat and sew through gathers and thread to secure them. Make a 5mm (⅛in) turn-up to right side at bottom edge. Put a scrap of filling into hat.

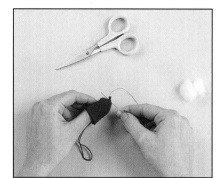

With seam to back, fit hat onto doll. **For the boy:** Cut 10 × 1cm (⅜in) lengths of yarn, push one end of each piece under hat front. **For the girl:** Cut 4 × 2cm (¾in) lengths, push both ends of each piece under hat to form loops on centre front head. When satisfied with position remove hat and hair, spread glue onto head and arrange hair.

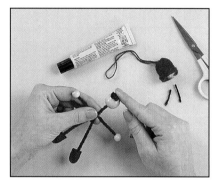

When glue is dry mark features onto doll with pencil before using the black pen for the eyes and the red for the mouth. Also colour cheeks red for the boy. Allow features to dry then glue edge of hat and place onto head over hair ends.

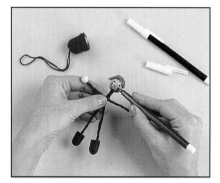

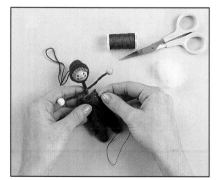

Oversew boy's trouser pieces together at sides A–B and inside leg seams C–D–C. Turn to right side out, easing through legs. Fit onto doll, add a scrap of filling to body of trousers and sew to pipe cleaners around waist. Make and fit girl's pantaloons in same way, then gather them at ankles and sew or glue lace to right side above gathers.

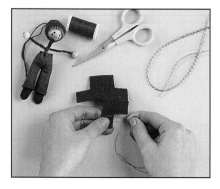

Cut boy's jacket for neck and front opening on solid lines E–E–J. Fold across shoulders N–N and sew side and underarm seams matching letters. Turn jacket through to right side out. Ease bead hands through arms to fit jacket onto the doll. Overlap fronts at neck and sew together between dots. Push scraps of filling under jacket around front and back shoulders.

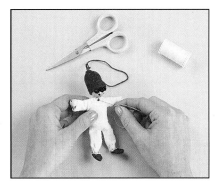

Cut a scrap of gold braid and glue to front. Fold feet to front at right angles to legs. Make girl's blouse in same way as jacket. Fit onto doll with opening at back. Add filling, overlap complete back opening and sew together. Gather and sew lower edge over pantaloon waist. Glue lace around neck and wrists and sew brooch bead to lace at front neck.

Glue or sew lace on wrong side to show below one long edge of skirt. On right side glue gold braid above bottom edge. Sew short skirt edges together. Sew long running stitches to gather waist. Fit skirt onto doll with seam at centre back and sew gathered edge to blouse at a high waistline. Glue or sew waistband, with join at back, to cover gathers.

Cut a fringe at scarf ends, tie scarf around boy's neck, glue one end to jacket front and leave other end free. Wrap shawl around girl, cross ends and glue in front.

Decorations only – not recommended for young children

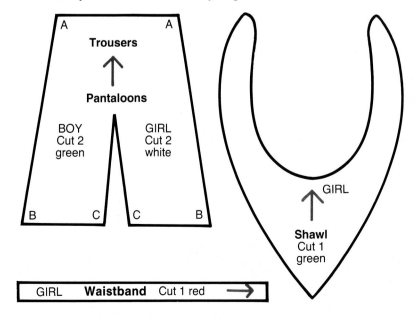

A   A

Trousers

↑

Pantaloons

BOY
Cut 2
green

GIRL
Cut 2
white

B   C   C   B

GIRL
↑
Shawl
Cut 1
green

GIRL	**Waistband**	Cut 1 red →

Actual height of dolls: 11cm (4¼in)

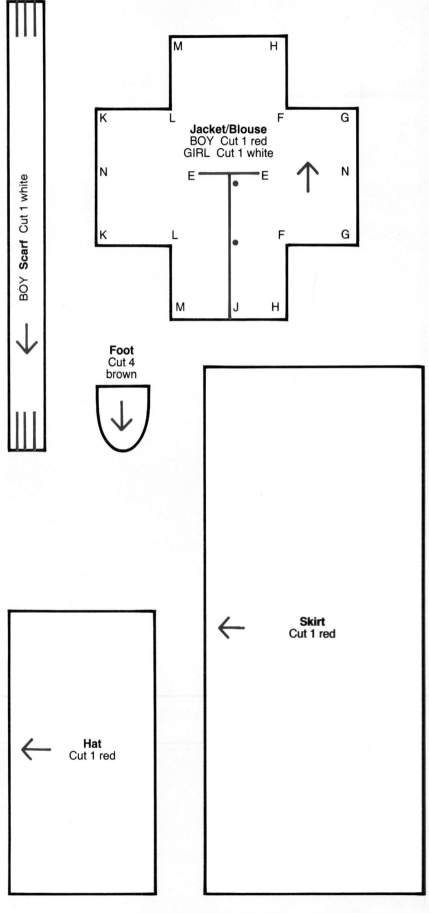

BOY **Scarf** Cut 1 white

M   H

K   L   F   G

Jacket/Blouse
BOY Cut 1 red
GIRL Cut 1 white

N   E — E   N

K   L   F   G

M   J   H

Foot
Cut 4
brown

Skirt
Cut 1 red

Hat
Cut 1 red

MATERIALS: 30cm × 50cm (12in × 20in) white fleece fabric; 3cm × 40cm (1¼in × 16in) blue felt or non-fray fabric; dark brown felt; light brown felt; black felt; orange felt; stiff cardboard; matching sewing threads; clear glue; bonding web; filling

Cut out all parts. Sew a running stitch all around edge of body base to gather it. Cut a 7cm (2¾in) diameter circle of stiff card as an inner base. Place card base in centre of wrong side of fabric, pull up gathers until card is tightly covered and fasten thread.

Stitch short edges of body together to form a tube. Turn body to right side out and turn under a small hem along one edge.

Fit base to body, with wrong sides facing and the body hem forming a rim around the base. Ladder stitch edge of base to the body hem.

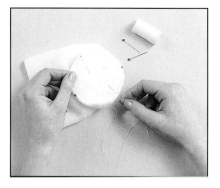

Sew a line of long running stitches around upper edge of body. Fill body with stuffing but do not pull up gathers. Leave body to one side.

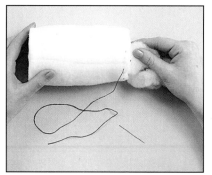

Stitch darts in head pieces. Stitch heads together leaving open neck edge. Turn head to the right side and sew running stitches around the neck on the broken lines.

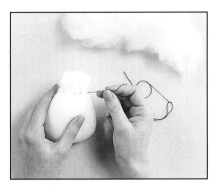

Fill head with stuffing moulding it to a round shape. Pull up gathers tightly, take several stitches through the neck and fasten thread.

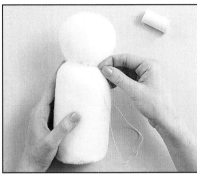

Insert neck into the body until gathers of head and body match and with body seam at the centre back of head. Pull up body neck gathers and secure thread. Ladder stitch the head to the body around the neck.

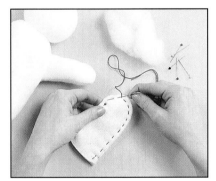

Stitch arms together in pairs, leaving open shoulder edges. Turn arms the right way out and fill with a little stuffing. Oversew open edges to enclose filling. Place arms against the snowman. Pin or baste them to body to check that you like the position. Sew right-hand arm close to body, the other to hold broom.

Sew running stitches along edge of each black felt eye, place scrap of filling in centre of eye, pull up stitches and secure thread. Sew eyes to head taking several stitches through head from eye to top back of head. Fold orange felt nose and oversew straight edges together, leaving open the curved edge.

Fill nose with stuffing and gather open edge. Sew to head, again taking stitches through the head. Cut a very narrow strip of black felt 2.5cm (1in) long for the mouth and glue or sew it to the head below the nose.

Cut two oversized pieces of brown felt for hat brim and bond them together with bonding web (see manufacturer's instructions) to make a firmer felt. Cut out brim. Oversew the two short edges of crown to make a tube. Turn crown, and seam, through to the other side. On outside of hat oversew the hat top piece to one edge of crown.

Insert crown into hat brim and oversew crown to brim on the underside around inside edge. Place hat onto the snowman's head and sew to body around brim and crown seam. Cut a fringe at both ends of scarf and tie around neck. Cut three small black felt buttons and sew or glue to front body.

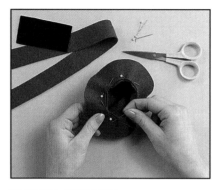

Roll brush handle along its length into a tight roll and oversew edge to the roll. Cut the fringe for the bristles. Roll bristles around one end of the handle and sew to secure. Bind top of bristles with a narrow strip of dark brown felt and with several turns of thread. Sew handle to snowman's arm.

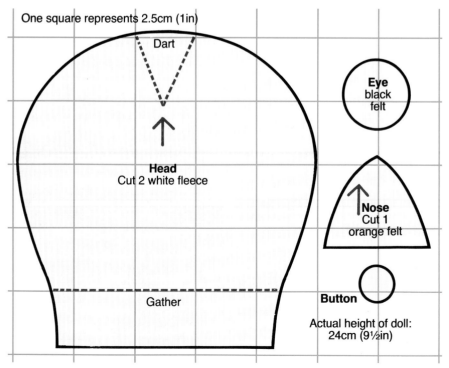

One square represents 2.5cm (1in)

Dart

Head
Cut 2 white fleece

Gather

Eye
black
felt

Nose
Cut 1
orange felt

Button

Actual height of doll:
24cm (9½in)

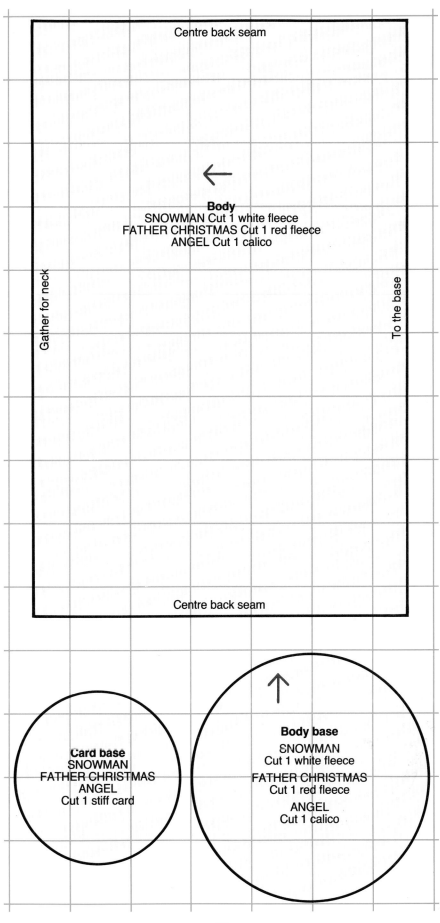

Centre back seam

←

Body
SNOWMAN Cut 1 white fleece
FATHER CHRISTMAS Cut 1 red fleece
ANGEL Cut 1 calico

Gather for neck

To the base

Centre back seam

↑

Card base
SNOWMAN
FATHER CHRISTMAS
ANGEL
Cut 1 stiff card

Body base
SNOWMAN
Cut 1 white fleece

FATHER CHRISTMAS
Cut 1 red fleece

ANGEL
Cut 1 calico

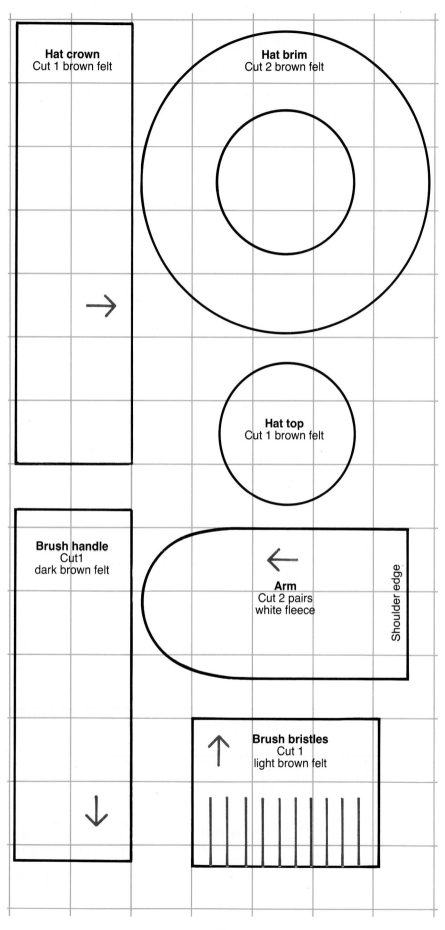

Hat crown
Cut 1 brown felt

Hat brim
Cut 2 brown felt

Hat top
Cut 1 brown felt

Brush handle
Cut1
dark brown felt

Arm
Cut 2 pairs
white fleece

Shoulder edge

Brush bristles
Cut 1
light brown felt

MATERIALS: 20cm × 112cm (8in × 44in) red fleece fabric; 10cm × 100cm (4in × 39in) white fleece fabric; 16cm × 30cm (6in × 12in) double thickness pink stockinette; long hair white fur fabric; brown felt; grey felt; black felt; stiff cardboard; red crayon; matching sewing threads; filling; a few tiny toys

Cut out all pieces. From white fleece cut bindings: cloak 6cm × 54cm (2¼in × 21in), hood 6cm × 27cm (2¼in × 10½in), two wrist bindings 4cm × 13cm (1½in × 5¼in). Follow Snowman instructions to make body and head, using red fleece for the body and pink stockinette for head.

Stitch dart in cloak A–B. Trim fabric close to seam. With right sides facing and raw edges even, stitch white fleece binding to cloak omitting neck edge C–A–C.

Turn binding over raw edges and slip stitch to wrong side. Sew a line of running stitches to gather neck of cloak. Pull up stitches to fit around body neck and fasten thread. Sew cloak to body around neck with the bound edges meeting at centre front C–A–C. Catch stitch cloak to body around lower front curves.

Bind straight edges of sleeves in same way as cloak edge. Fold arm along the broken line on pattern and stitch underarm seam around curved edge to wrist. Turn arm to right side out and fill softly with stuffing.

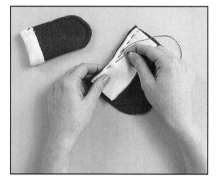

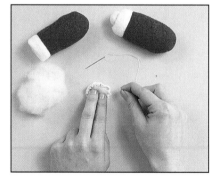

To make the hand, sew a running thread around edges of a double circle of stockinette. Add filling to centre of circle, pull up stitches tightly and fasten thread. Push raw edges of hand into sleeve and sew to wrist binding. Make second hand and sew into sleeve. Pin sleeves to cloak. When satisfied with their position sew them firmly through cloak to body.

Make grey felt eyes in same way as hands and pin to head. Cut out mouth hole in beard and trim fur pile along upper mouth to make a moustache. Pin beard to body and lightly mark positions for mouth and nose. Brush hair pile to one long edge, turn under and slip stitch this edge to wrong side.

Pin hair to head with fold to face. When you are happy with the expression, remove beard and mark a red mouth and nose with crayon. Sew eyes, beard and hair to head. Bind hood edge as you did for cloak. Stitch hood seam D–A. Turn hood to right side out and fit onto head.

Turn under hood neck edge to just cover raw edge of cloak. Sew hood to cloak around the neck C–A–C, with the bound edges meeting at centre front under beard. Sew black boots to lower centre front of body.

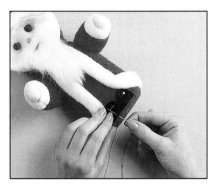

Stitch sack pieces together leaving open the straight edges. Turn sack right side out and lightly fill with stuffing. Sew a line of running stitches around neck of sack to gather, pull up stitches loosely and fasten thread. Add a few tiny toys to top of sack. Stitch sack to hand.

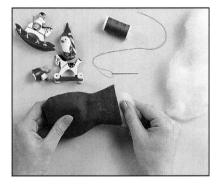

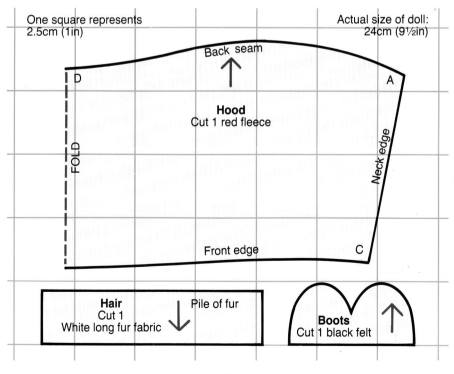

One square represents 2.5cm (1in)

Actual size of doll: 24cm (9½in)

Back seam

D — A

Hood
Cut 1 red fleece

FOLD

Neck edge

Front edge — C

Hair
Cut 1
White long fur fabric

Pile of fur

Boots
Cut 1 black felt

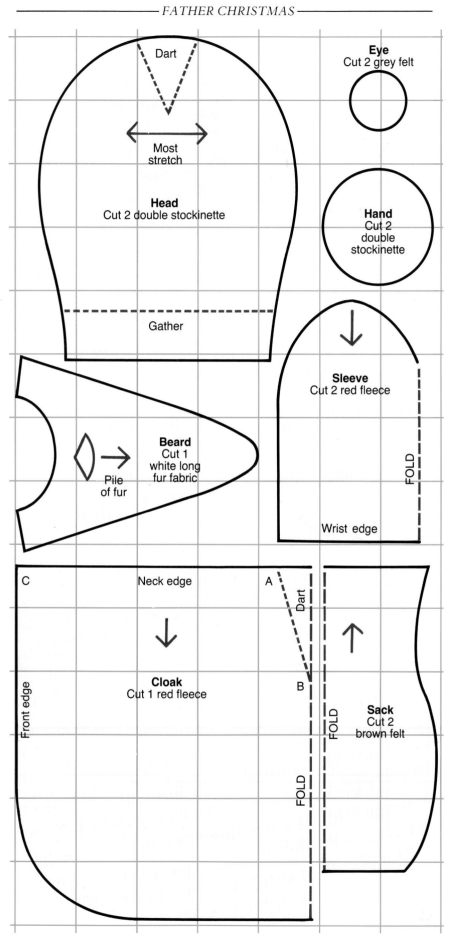

Dart

Eye
Cut 2 grey felt

Most stretch

Head
Cut 2 double stockinette

Hand
Cut 2 double stockinette

Gather

Sleeve
Cut 2 red fleece

Beard
Cut 1 white long fur fabric

Pile of fur

FOLD

Wrist edge

C

Neck edge

A

Dart

B

Cloak
Cut 1 red fleece

Front edge

FOLD

FOLD

Sack
Cut 2 brown felt

MATERIALS: *20cm × 80cm (8in × 31½in) unbleached calico; 18cm × 24cm (7in × 9in) pale pink felt; 120cm × 3.5cm (48in × 1½in) cream cotton lace; 1.60m (72in) narrow gold braid; heavyweight interfacing; 30cm (12in) blonde mohair dolls' hair; scrap of black felt; bonding web; red crayon; filling; stiff card; gold faced card; craft glue; pinking shears*

Cut out all pieces. Follow instructions for Snowman to make body and head using calico for body and pink felt for head. Cut 50cm (20in) lace. With joins at centre back, sew in pleats around lower edge of body, to make a frill. Cut more lace to fit around body without pleats and sew it above lace frill with decorative edge covering previous pleated edge.

Sew gold braid around top edge of lace band with a second piece above it. Cut 30cm (12in) lace and sew a running stitch along the straight edge. Pull up stitches to fit around neck and sew to cover head and body seam, with the join at the back. Sew neck frill to body at centre front.

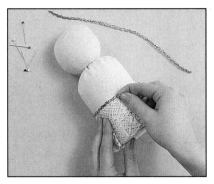

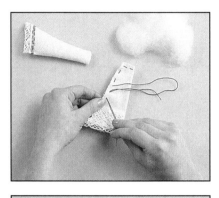

Turn under a narrow hem at sleeve wrist A–B–A. Baste lace to wrong side with lace edge just showing on the right side. Stitch gold braid to right side on hem line through calico and lace. With right sides together fold sleeve B–B and stitch seam B–C–A. Turn sleeve to right side out and fill softly with stuffing. Make the second sleeve.

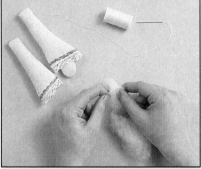

Stitch hands together in pairs leaving open straight edges. Turn to right side out and add a little filling. Place hand into sleeve between B and A and sew through sleeve hem to secure. Complete second sleeve. Pin both sleeves onto body at sides and back with the hands almost meeting at centre front. Sew them to body, leaving front sleeves and hands free.

Spread glue onto head from hair line to centre back and allow to dry slightly. Tease mohair into a single layer and gently arrange on head. When glue is dry secure hair to head with stitches. Cut gold braid to fit around head, sew ends together and fit. Cut two black felt eyes (use a paper punch) and glue or sew to head. Mark mouth and cheeks with crayon.

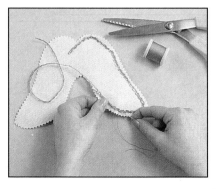

Cut an oversize piece of calico for wings. Bond this to interfacing (see manufacturer's instructions) and cut out one pair of wings with pinking shears. Sew gold braid inside right side edge beginning at lower centre of wings. Sew to body back to cover ends of arms. Cut a piece of gold faced card 8cm × 4cm (3in × 1½in). Fold card down centre and glue between hands.

One square represents 2.5cm (1in)
Actual height of doll: 20cm (8in)

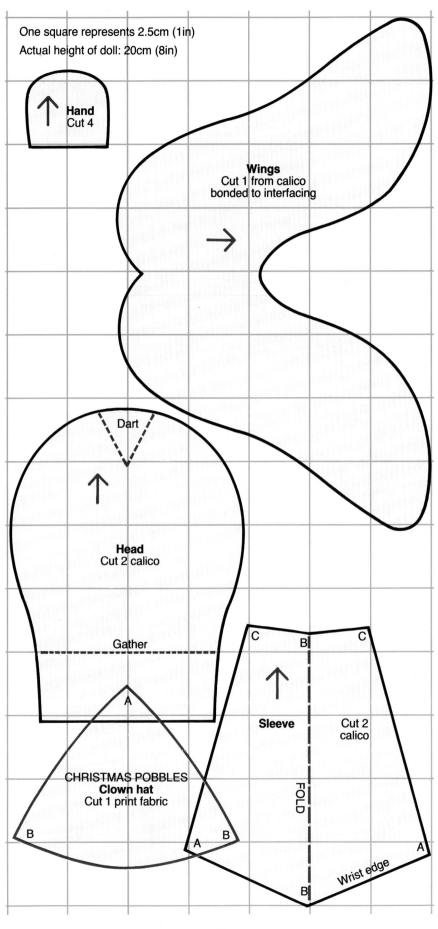

Hand
Cut 4

Wings
Cut 1 from calico
bonded to interfacing

Dart

Head
Cut 2 calico

Gather

A

C B C

Sleeve

Cut 2
calico

CHRISTMAS POBBLES
Clown hat
Cut 1 print fabric

B

A B

FOLD

B

A

B

Wrist edge

THE CHRISTMAS POBBLES

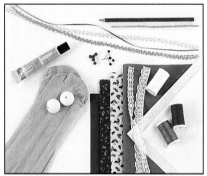

MATERIALS: *Printed cotton fabric; lining fabric; white or green fabric; decorative braids, narrow lace, narrow red ribbon; 1 × 25mm (1in) diameter cotton craft ball, 2 black map pins 1 flesh colour pipe cleaner for each doll; flesh colour nylon tights; matching sewing threads; tiny red pom poms or beads; 5cm (2in) diameter circle thin card; filling; red crayon; clear drying craft glue; pinking shears*

For either doll: Cut body circle 18cm (7in) diameter and sleeves 13cm × 5cm (5in × 2in) in print fabric; inner Body circle 18cm (7in) diameter in lining fabric; body base circle 5cm (2in) diameter in card. **For the girl:** Cut hat circle 8cm (3in) diameter in white fabric. **For the clown:** Cut hat (page 65) from print fabric; ruff 13cm × 2cm (5in x ¾in) in green using pinking shears.

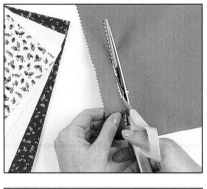

For either doll: Sew long running stitches around edge of inner body circle. Mould filling to make a ball of about 7.5cm (3in) diameter and place in centre of inner body. Pull up stitches to gather edge tightly and secure. Glue card base to cover stitches. Gather edge of body circle. Place card base to centre of wrong side of body. Pull up stitches.

66

Cover cotton craft ball with a double layer of nylon tights. The hole in ball should be at the neck. Cut a square of nylon and stretch over ball gathering at neck, sew through tights and bind with thread to form a neck. Trim nylon if necessary. Push neck into body gathers and sew through body and neck to secure head. Sew braid around body.

For the girl: Cut 20cm (8in) narrow lace. **For the clown:** Use the green ruff. Sew short edges together and gather one long edge. Place circle over head with join at the back, pull up tightly around neck and secure thread. Tie narrow ribbon around clown's neck with bow at front.

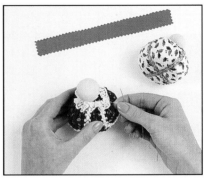

Press ½cm (¼in) to wrong side on all edges of sleeves. With wrong sides facing fold sleeve along centre length and slip stitch long edges together. Fold over 1.5cm (⅝in) at ends of pipe cleaner to make hands. Slip arms into sleeve, gather and sew fabric around wrists. Sew braid at wrists. Place arms around body with back under ruff and sew leaving front arms free.

Sew lace around edge of right side of girl's hat. Sew running stitches 1.5cm (⅝in) from fabric edge to gather. Pull up stitches until hat fits head, add filling to crown and sew hat to head around gathers. Sew ribbon above gathers and tie with bow in front. Sew or glue pom pom or bead to centre of neck lace.

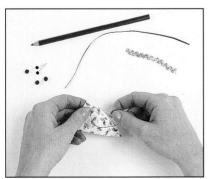

Sew clown's hat seam A–B. Turn to right side. Fill with stuffing and sew to head around edge. Sew braid to cover edge, sew or glue one pom pom or bead to front and three to body centre front. Glue back of map pins and press into head. Mark mouth in red crayon. Cut 20cm (8in) narrow ribbon, fold in centre, sew ends to body and loop to back of head to balance doll.

MATERIALS: 30cm × 68cm (12in × 27in) double thickness pink stockinette; 40cm × 114cm (16in × 45in) green spotted fabric; 40cm × 96cm (16in × 38in) blue spotted fabric; 20cm × 90cm (8in × 36in) yellow fabric; 30cm × 30cm (12in × 12in) red felt; scraps of white, blue and black felts; 70cm (28in) red ric-rac braid; red and black stranded embroidery threads; black soft embroidery thread; matching sewing threads; narrow elastic and bodkin; double knitting yarn; filling; clear drying craft glue

Cut all pieces from patterns. From stockinette cut two legs 20cm × 11cm (8in × 4in) and two arms 17cm × 9cm (7in × 3½in), with most stretch across shorter measurements. From yellow fabric cut one ruff 70cm × 16cm (28in × 6in) and one circle of 6cm (2⅜in) diameter.

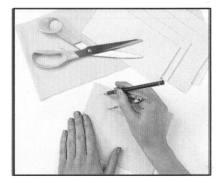

On right side of body stockinette mark a light pencil line to indicate neck gathers. Stitch together edges A–B, to form a tube. Turn body to right side out. Sew a line of long running stitches on pencil line but do not pull up stitches.

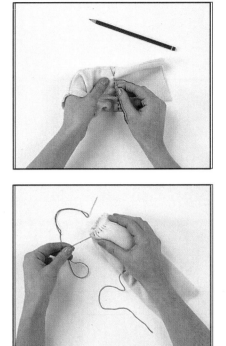

Fill head with stuffing until it has a circumference of 23cm (9in). To give a good shape to head, mould filling into a ball in your hands before placing in head. Sew a line of running stitches to gather top of head. Pull up stitches until stockinette is tightly bunched, oversew across gathers and secure thread. Add a little filling to neck.

Pull up running stitches until the neck measures 10cm (4in) in circumference, take several stitches through neck and fasten thread. Fill body. Fold lower edge of body matching B and C; the seam will be at centre back of doll. Turn in raw edges and oversew together.

Fold a leg along length. Stitch long edge and one short edge. Turn leg to right side out and fill lightly with stuffing. Sew long running stitches around open edge. Pull up stitches to tightly gather fabric and fasten thread.

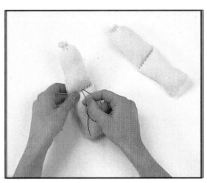

Flatten leg in centre of length and by hand make a line of stab stitches across leg through the fabric and filling to make leg bend. Make second leg.

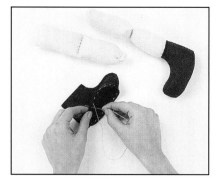

Stitch boots together in pairs D–E and F–G. Stitch boot soles into boots E–G. Turn boots to right side out and fill with stuffing. Insert gathered end of leg into boot and sew top of boot to leg. Check that the second boot and leg are made to the same length as first one.

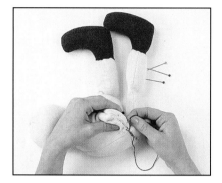

Place legs to lower edge of body with fronts facing and leg seams meeting at body centre C. Firmly oversew legs to body.

Stitch a 2.5cm (1in) hem to wrong side of hat H–H. Fold hat matching H and H and stitch seam J–H. Turn to right side out. Sew running stitches around edge of yellow fabric circle. Add filling to centre of circle and pull up stitches, shape it into a ball and secure thread.

Sew bobble to front of hat point. Fill hat lightly with stuffing and fit onto head with lower back seam edge almost at centre back neck gathers. Stitch hat hem to head at front.

For the hair, wind 10 strands of yarn around two fingers and sew them together at one place. Cut yarn ends close to these stitches. Make twelve bunches of yarn and sew six to each side of face at hat hem.

Glue the white outer eyes in place with the blue inner eyes and black eye centres on top of them. With a pencil lightly mark curved mouth and embroider with two strands of red embroidery thread. Glue red cheek circles at the ends of mouth.

Sew features in place with stitches taken from back of head, under hat edge through head and felt features. Then take needle back through felt part and head and fasten thread at back head. A small straight black stitch at centre top of blue inner eye will add to clown's expression. Stitch back hat hem to head.

Stitch hems to wrong side at suit legs K–K. Stitch blue suit piece to green suit piece at centre front L–M and at centre back L–M. Stitch inside leg seams K–M–K. Turn suit to right side out and fit onto doll. Turn under neck edge and sew a line of running stitches around folded edge to gather it.

Pull up stitches and sew gathers to doll's neck, checking that suit centre seams at L are central to body. Sew running stitches on broken lines to gather lower edge of each leg. Sew gathers to top of boots. Work a black cross stitch in centre of each red felt button using black soft embroidery thread. Sew 'buttons' to suit front centre seam.

Make up stockinette arms as for legs. Stitch hands together in pairs leaving open straight edges N–P. Turn to right side out. On broken lines top stitch finger markings. Place a little filling into palm of hands. Insert gathered ends of arms into hands N–P and sew in place.

Stitch a 1cm (⅜in) hem at one edge of a sleeve N–N. Stitch edges of sleeve together Q–N and turn sleeve to right side out. Turn seam allowance on remaining edge Q–Q to wrong side and sew a line of long running stitches around this folded edge to gather it.

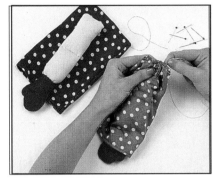

Fit arm into sleeve with gathers to the shoulder. Pull up running stitches gathering sleeve to fit upper edge of arm. Arrange sleeve gathers evenly around arm, with sleeve seam to the side of arm. Sew gathers to arm covering all the pink stockinette.

Sew running stitches on broken lines to gather sleeve at wrist, pull up stitches and sew gathers to hand. Make second sleeve. Join arms to body, with thumbs to the front, just below suit neck gathers Q–Q. Firmly oversew tops of arms through suit to body.

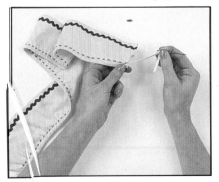

With right sides facing fold ruff along centre length. Stitch together long edges. Turn ruff through to right side out. Press with seam to one edge. Top stitch 1cm (⅜in) from this edge to form a channel. Stitch ric-rac braid to right side of folded edge. Thread elastic through channel and sew one end to secure it.

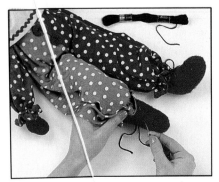

Pull up gathers to fit clown's neck and sew elastic with thread to fasten. Trim excess. Stitch short ends of ruff together. Fit ruff onto doll with seam at centre back. With black soft embroidery thread and a long needle, thread 'laces' through boots. Knot threads and tie in a firm bow to prevent them being pulled out.

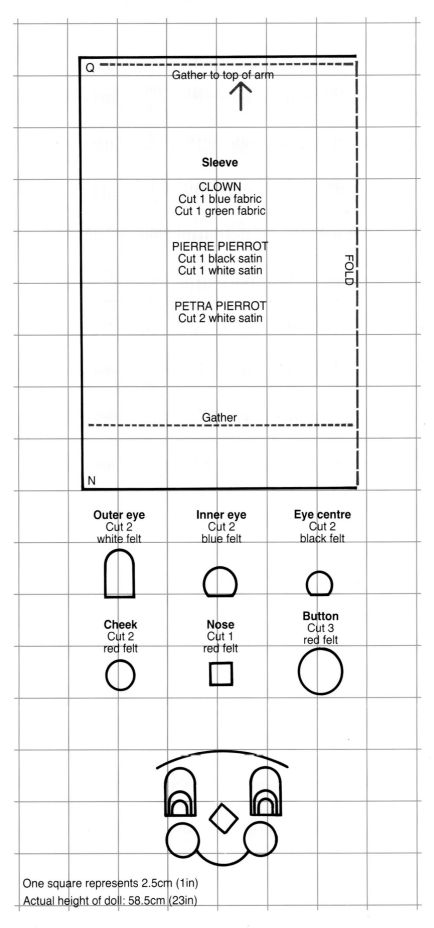

Q

Gather to top of arm

Sleeve

CLOWN
Cut 1 blue fabric
Cut 1 green fabric

PIERRE PIERROT
Cut 1 black satin
Cut 1 white satin

PETRA PIERROT
Cut 2 white satin

FOLD

Gather

N

Outer eye
Cut 2
white felt

Inner eye
Cut 2
blue felt

Eye centre
Cut 2
black felt

Cheek
Cut 2
red felt

Nose
Cut 1
red felt

Button
Cut 3
red felt

One square represents 2.5cm (1in)
Actual height of doll: 58.5cm (23in)

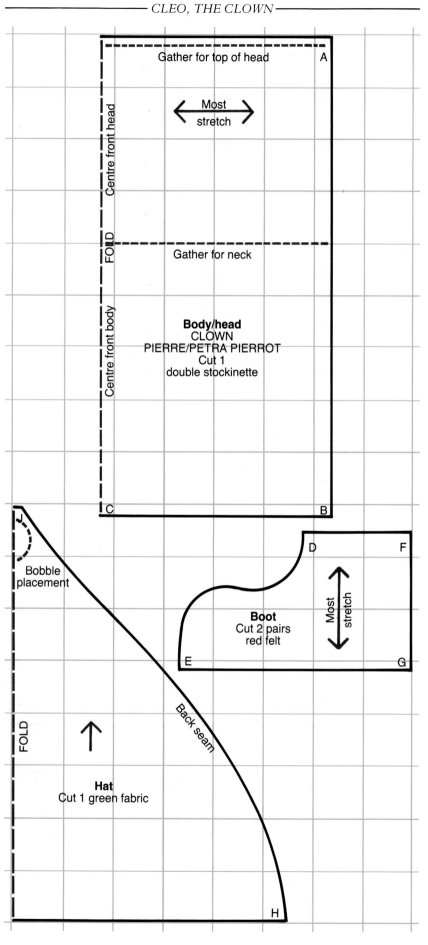

Gather for top of head — A

Most stretch

Centre front head

FOLD

Gather for neck

Centre front body

Body/head
CLOWN
PIERRE/PETRA PIERROT
Cut 1
double stockinette

C — B

Bobble placement

Boot
Cut 2 pairs
red felt

Most stretch

D — F

E — G

Back seam

FOLD

Hat
Cut 1 green fabric

H

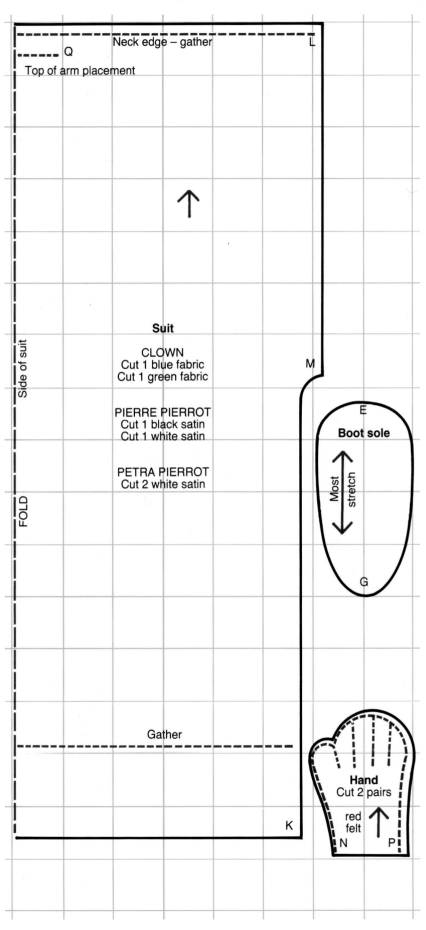

Neck edge – gather

Q

Top of arm placement

L

Side of suit

FOLD

Suit

CLOWN
Cut 1 blue fabric
Cut 1 green fabric

PIERRE PIERROT
Cut 1 black satin
Cut 1 white satin

PETRA PIERROT
Cut 2 white satin

M

E

Boot sole

Most stretch

G

Gather

K

Hand
Cut 2 pairs

red felt

N

P

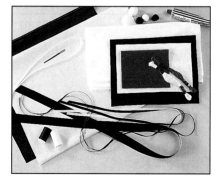

MATERIALS: 30cm × 68cm (12in × 27in) double thickness white stockinette; 50cm × 60cm (20in × 24in) black satin (polyester), 70cm × 90cm (28in × 36in) white satin; 30cm × 40cm (12in × 16in) black felt, 16cm × 16cm (6in × 6in) white felt, scrap of red felt; 60cm × 3mm (24in × 1/8in), 24cm × 7mm (9in × 1/4in), 70cm × 25mm (28in × 1in) black satin ribbon; 24cm × 7mm (9in × 1/4in) white satin ribbon; 2 × 30mm (11/4in) white pom poms, 2 × 18mm (3/4in) black pom poms, 1 × 18mm (3/4in) white pom pom; red and white stranded embroidery threads; matching sewing threads; narrow elastic and bodkin; filling; clear drying glue

Cut out all pieces from patterns. From white satin also cut ruff 10cm × 60cm (4in × 24in). From stockinette cut two legs 20cm × 11cm (8in × 4in) and two arms 17cm × 9cm (7in × 3½in) with most stretch across shorter measurements. Follow steps 2–8 of Clown instructions to make body. Note that the boots are a different shape.

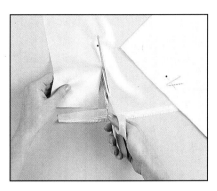

Stitch front hat to centre hat J–H, matching dots. Stitch dart in back hat. Stitch centre hat to back hat K–L, matching triangles. Turn hat to right side out, place a little filling in centre of hat and fit onto head. Sew edge of hat to head.

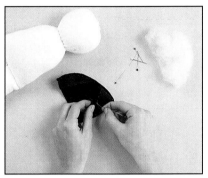

Place eyes, cheeks and mouth on face. Mark position of nose and eyebrows. This can be done with pins, then a light pencil line. When satisfied with the expression, glue or sew felt features to fabric.

Using two strands of embroidery thread work two straight red stitches for each eyebrow and two tiny stitches for nose. With two strands of white thread stitch highlights onto eyes.

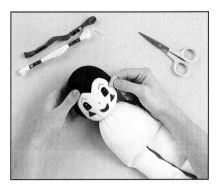

Follow step 14 from Clown instructions, stitching black satin suit piece to white satin suit piece. Pull up running stitches around folded neck edge, checking that suit centre seams at L are central to body. Sew running stitches on broken lines to gather lower edge of legs. Sew gathers to top of boots.

Make up white stockinette arms and white felt hands – see step 16 in Clown's instructions for full details.

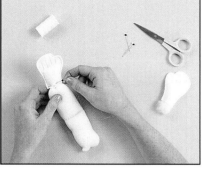

Follow steps 17–19 of Clown's instructions to make up sleeves – one in black and the other in white satin – and attach arms to body.
Note: Black-sleeved arm is attached to white side of suit, white-sleeved to black half of suit.

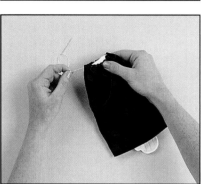

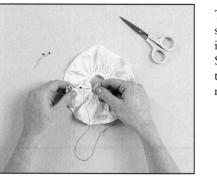

Stitch 1cm ($\frac{3}{8}$in) hem at one long edge of the ruff. Stitch a 13mm ($\frac{1}{2}$in) hem at the opposite long edge to form a channel for the elastic. On right side stitch 3mm ($\frac{1}{8}$in) black ribbon over first hem stitches.

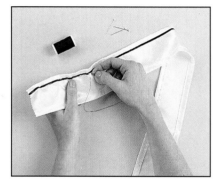

Thread elastic through ruff channel, stitching one end to fabric to secure it. Pull up fabric to fit doll's neck. Stitch two short edges of ruff together. Trim excess elastic and neaten seam. Fit ruff onto doll.

Tie a 2.5cm (1in) black ribbon around neck with bow at front. Sew a band of contrast 7mm ($\frac{1}{4}$in) ribbon around each wrist and ankle with the joins at the backs. Sew two black and one white 18mm ($\frac{3}{4}$in) pom pom evenly spaced to suit centre front seam. Sew one 30mm ($1\frac{1}{4}$in) white pom pom to each boot.

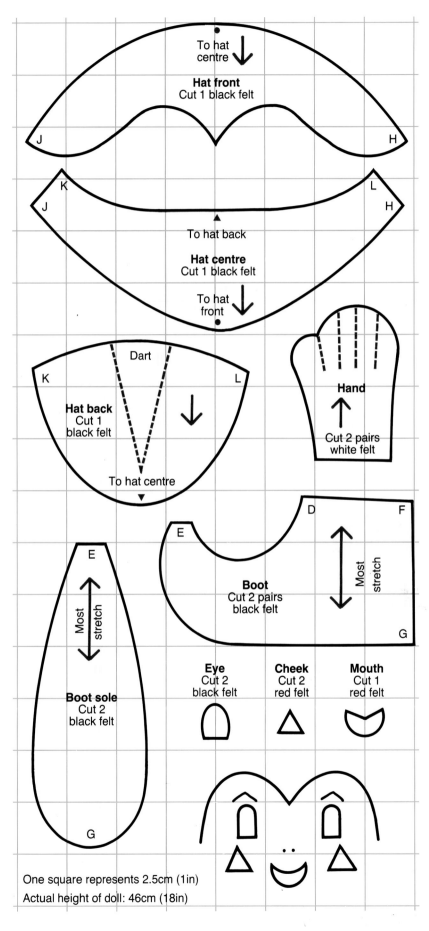

To hat centre

Hat front
Cut 1 black felt

J

H

K

L

J

H

To hat back

Hat centre
Cut 1 black felt

To hat front

Dart

K

L

Hat back
Cut 1
black felt

To hat centre

Hand

Cut 2 pairs
white felt

D

F

E

Most stretch

Boot
Cut 2 pairs
black felt

G

E

Most stretch

Boot sole
Cut 2
black felt

Eye
Cut 2
black felt

Cheek
Cut 2
red felt

Mouth
Cut 1
red felt

G

One square represents 2.5cm (1in)

Actual height of doll: 46cm (18in)

MATERIALS: 30cm × 68cm (12in × 27in) double thickness white stockinette; 80cm × 100cm (31in × 39in) white satin; 26cm × 26cm (10in × 10in) black felt; 16cm × 14cm (6in × 5½in) white felt; Scrap of red felt; 270cm × 3mm (106in × ⅛in) black satin ribbon; 100cm × 2.5cm (39in × 1in) black satin ribbon; 120cm (47in) black ric-rac braid; 4 × 30mm (1¼in) white pom poms; 1 × 18mm (¾in) black pom pom; narrow elastic and bodkin; red and white embroidery threads; filling; clear drying craft glue

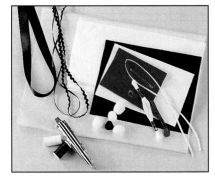

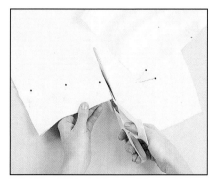

Cut all pieces from patterns. From satin also cut the skirt 28cm × 76cm (11in × 30in) and ruff 7cm × 40cm (3in × 16in). From stockinette cut legs and arms as for the Clown doll.

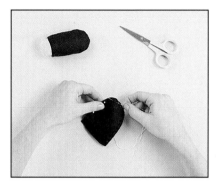

Follow steps 2–8 of Clown instructions. Note that the shoes are a different shape. Stitch shoes together in pairs leaving open straight edge X–Y. Turn shoes to right side out and fill with stuffing. Insert gathered end of leg into shoe and sew shoe to leg. Check that second shoe and leg are made to the same length as first one.

Stitch front hat to centre hat R–S, matching dots. Stitch dart in back hat and stitch centre hat to back hat W–T, matching triangles.

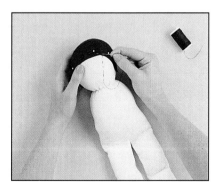

Turn hat to right side out, place a little filling in centre of hat and fit onto head. Sew edge of hat to head.

Follow steps 3 and 4 of Pierre Pierrot instructions for features but use the girl's patterns.

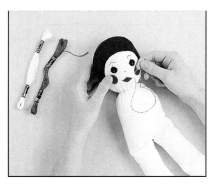

Follow steps 14–19 of Clown instructions with these alterations: use white satin for both suit pieces and sleeves. After stitching hem at sleeve wrist N–N, stitch 3mm (⅛in) black ribbon to right side of sleeve over hem stitches.

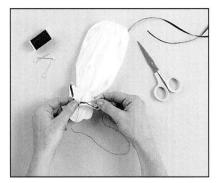

Stitch a 15mm (⅝in) hem to wrong side at one long edge of skirt. On right side stitch a band of 3mm (⅛in) ribbon over hem stitches with a band of ric-rac braid above it. To form a channel for waist elastic, stitch a 13mm (½in) double hem at opposite long edge.

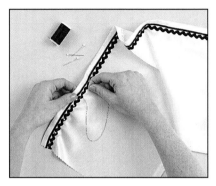

Thread through elastic and sew one end to fabric to secure it. Pull up elastic to fit doll's waist. Stitch short edges of skirt together including elastic. Fit skirt onto doll. Arrange suit to make an evenly gathered bodice and sew skirt waist to suit and body.

Tie a 2.5cm (1in) ribbon sash around waist to cover top of skirt. Catch stitch lower edge of sash to skirt and take a few stitches through bow to secure it.

Sew a 30mm (1¼in) white pom pom to the front of each shoe. Cut two 30cm (12in) lengths of 3mm (⅛in) wide black ribbon and tie around suit legs, to cover ankle gathers with bows at front. Sew remaining pom poms, two white and one black, to hat.

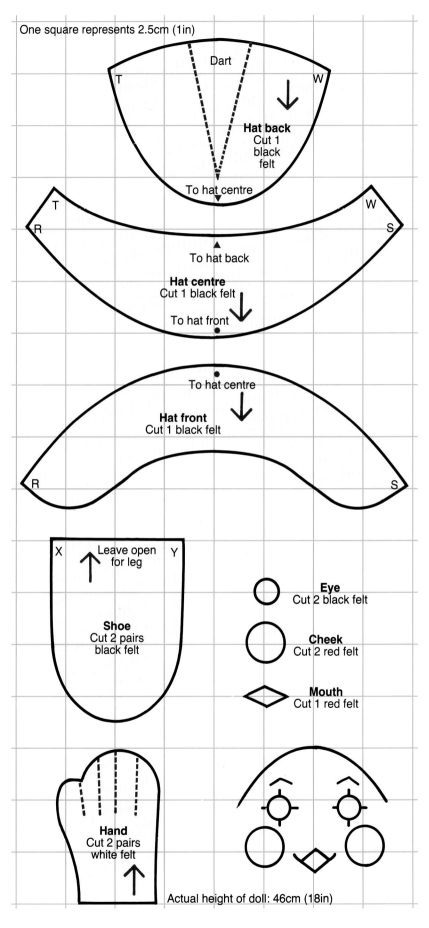

One square represents 2.5cm (1in)

Dart

T   W

Hat back
Cut 1
black
felt

To hat centre

T   W
R   S

To hat back

Hat centre
Cut 1 black felt

To hat front

To hat centre

Hat front
Cut 1 black felt

R   S

X   Leave open
for leg   Y

Shoe
Cut 2 pairs
black felt

Eye
Cut 2 black felt

Cheek
Cut 2 red felt

Mouth
Cut 1 red felt

Hand
Cut 2 pairs
white felt

Actual height of doll: 46cm (18in)

MATERIALS: For one doll – paper ball 30mm (1¼in) diameter; two white pipe cleaners; 1 skein of soft embroidery cotton; 12cm × 6cm (5in × 2in) wide broderie anglaise; 10cm × 40cm (4in × 16in) fine print fabric; scrap of pink fabric; 50cm × 3mm (20in × ⅛in) ribbon; 50cm × 6mm (20in × ¼in) ribbon; 3 daisy trimming motifs; matching sewing threads; scrap of filling; thin and thick card; red and white poster paint; black fine fibre-tip pen; fine paint brush; clear drying craft glue; 1 × 16cm (6in) square green felt to cover base; lace, flowers, cake decorations

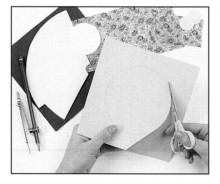

Cut out all parts. Cut two 3cm (1¼in) circles of pink fabric for the hands. From thin card cut one circle of 6cm (2⅜in) diameter for the body base. From thick card cut one circle 12cm (4¾in) diameter for the base. At each stage allow glue to dry before proceeding. 1cm (⅜in) seam is included.

Score along curved broken line on body cone with scissor points. Snip lower edge of body cone evenly to scored line. Overlap and glue body edges to form a cone with a 6cm (2⅜in) diameter open base. Bend snipped edge to inside. Glue outer face of snipped card and press to smaller body base circle.

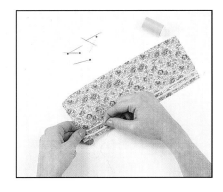

Stitch a 1cm (⅜in) hem at one long skirt edge. Stitch two ribbon bands to right side at hem. Stitch short edges together.

Sew a line of long running stitches along remaining long raw edge. Pull up stitches, fit skirt onto cone with hem level with base and secure thread. Glue skirt gathers to cone just below apex. For the apron, hem short edges of broderie anglaise. Gather raw edge and glue apron to top front of skirt with gathered edges even.

Cut one pipe cleaner to 12cm (4¾in) and fold each end to form hands. Gather edges of circles of pink fabric and sew over hands.

Press single hems to wrong side of each short edge of sleeve. With wrong sides facing fold sleeve along centre length A–B. Stitch seam C–D, leaving open in centre between dots. Turn sleeve to right side out. Slip arms into sleeves. Turn under raw edges and sew wrists to hands. Push a tiny scrap of filling into each arm.

Cut tiny hole in sleeve at E. Place centre of sleeves over body and glue open edges to cover skirt top. Tie a 6mm (¼in) ribbon sash around waist with bow at back. Sew or glue in place.

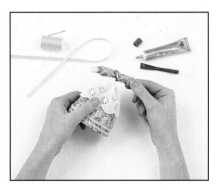

To make head, fold a pipe cleaner in half and glue fold into hole in paper ball. Fix pipe cleaner into a block of florist's foam or otherwise secure it upright. Mix paint to make a pale pink. Paint the ball and pipe cleaner neck.

When paint is dry, spread glue over ball from front and side hair lines to back hair line. Allow glue to become tacky. For yellow-haired doll, cut 20cm (8in) strands of soft embroidery cotton. Place across head working from front to back, laying strands close to each other. Fold centre back strand in half to complete covering head.

If making a fringe for the dark-haired doll, cut six 2.5cm (1in) strands of soft embroidery cotton. Glue one end of each strand to centre of head with strands covering centre of face. Cut longer strands, as before, placing them across glued head covering fixed ends of fringe. When dry, trim fringe and hair.

For the doll with plaits, cut 25cm (10in) strands of soft embroidery cotton, place across glued head bringing each strand to front of doll. Allow to dry. Cut short strands and glue to centre front hair line if it appears too high. Divide strands at centre back and plait at front of doll. Tie ends with ribbon or thread and trim strands.

Lightly mark features with a pencil. Paint a dark pink mouth and nose and paler pink rosy cheeks. Mark eyes and eyebrows. It helps to practice on a piece of paper before painting doll. Push pipe cleaner neck through hole in sleeves and into cone. Leave a short neck and glue in place. Glue daisy motifs around neck to cover join.

Bend or sew doll's hand around chosen decoration. To make posy of flowers, sew a line of running stitches along straight edge of 7.5cm (3in) narrow lace. Pull up stitches and sew lace around several small artificial flowers. Trim flower stems if necessary and sew posy to doll's hand.

To make base, glue one face of larger card circle and place onto centre of green felt. Snip excess felt to card and glue to underside. Glue flower heads around edges of base and doll to centre.

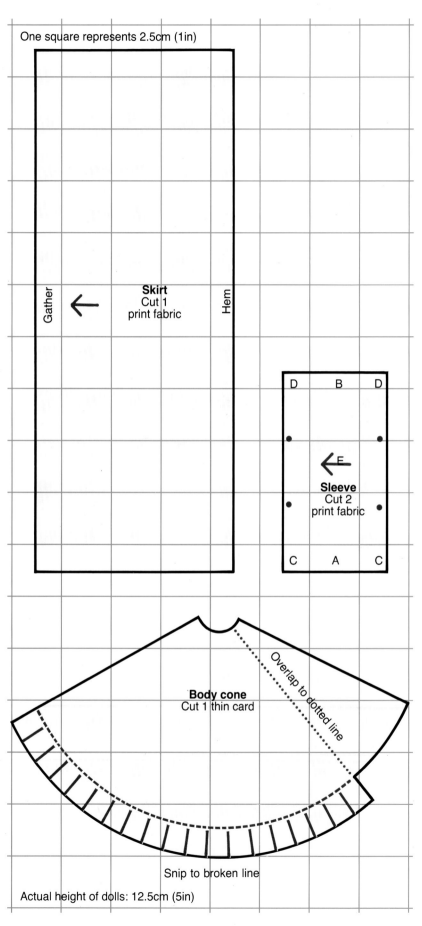

One square represents 2.5cm (1in)

Gather

Skirt
Cut 1
print fabric

Hem

D   B   D

E

Sleeve
Cut 2
print fabric

C   A   C

Body cone
Cut 1 thin card

Overlap to dotted line

Snip to broken line

Actual height of dolls: 12.5cm (5in)

SIMON AND SALLY SOCK

MATERIALS: For one doll – 1 man's towelling sock; small doll's vinyl face; 36cm × 7mm (14in × ¼in) wide satin ribbon; 20cm (8in) narrow broiderie anglaise edging or lace; 3 daisy motifs; 70cm (28in) fine yellow or brown yarn; matching sewing threads; filling

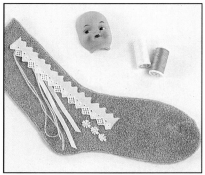

Turn sock to wrong side out and cut along all solid lines as shown on diagram. Discard ribbing.

Oversew all cut edges to prevent fraying. Open out body section to bring A–A and fold doll's legs along centre lines B–C–D.

Stitch doll leg seams C–A–C curving lower edges. Trim fabric around curves. Turn body through to right side out.

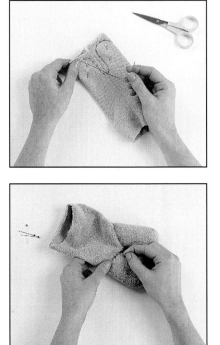

Fill legs with stuffing and stitch across top of them at a slight angle to allow them to bend. Fill body.

Sew a line of long running stitches close to open edge, pull up stitches until opening is slightly smaller than doll's face and securely fasten thread.

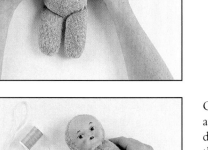

Oversew face to cover opening, adding extra filling behind it as you do so. Sew running stitches around the body below the head, pull up thread until gathers pull in body to form a neck, then secure it.

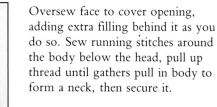

For the hair, wind yarn around two fingers to form loops and sew these to fabric above centre of face.

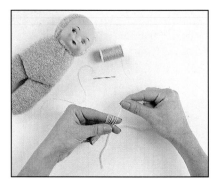

With wrong sides facing and raw edges even, fold brim section along its centre, matching F–F and G–G. Oversew raw edges together adding a little filling as you work to make brim into a soft 'ring doughnut' roll.

Fit brim around face with seam to the back and sew to body. Cut ribbon into two lengths, sew one end of each through brim at sides of neck and tie in a bow. Take several stitches through bow to prevent it coming undone.

Sew broiderie anglaise or lace around neck with the joins at the back. Sew three daisy trimmings down centre front of body.

Fold arms along centres H–K, matching J–J. Stitch seam, curving it as shown on broken line and leaving open J–K. Trim fabric around curves. Turn arms through to right side out and fill lightly with stuffing.

To form the hands, secure threads and wind them around arms 2.5cm (1in) from closed ends. Turn in open edges and sew arms to body.

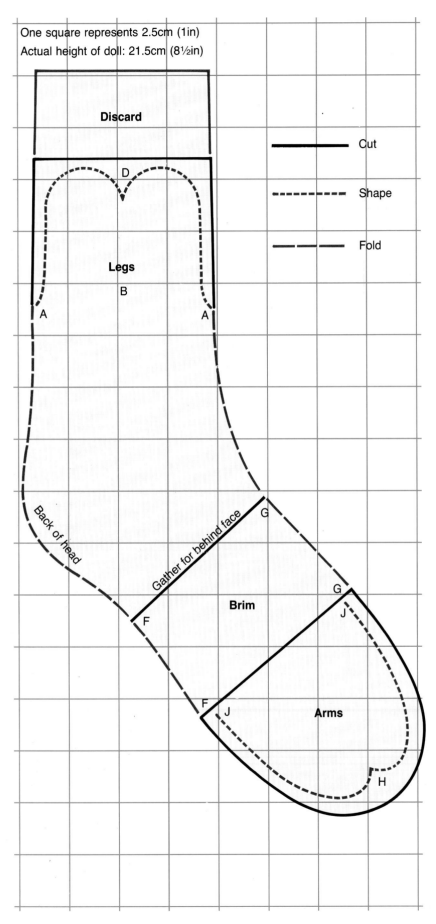

One square represents 2.5cm (1in)
Actual height of doll: 21.5cm (8½in)

Discard

Cut

Shape

Fold

Legs

D

B

A   A

Back of head

Gather for behind face

G

G

F

Brim

J

F
J   Arms

H

PRETTY PETULA

MATERIALS: *Body – 40cm × 90cm (16in × 36in) pink calico; 18cm × 18cm (7in × 7in) lightweight stretch; interfacing; 18cm ×18cm (7in × 7in) tracing paper; 30cm × 6cm (12in × 2in) wide lace for socks; 23cm × 23cm (9in × 9in) blue felt; 50g (1½oz) ball brown 4-ply knitting yarn; 16cm (6in) brown narrow tape; blue, black, white, brown and pink stranded embroidery threads; pink and light brown crayons; 5cm × 7cm (2in × 2¾in) stiff card; filling. Dress and pants – 50cm × 90cm (20in × 36in) fine print fabric; 220cm (87in) decorative pre-gathered lace; 140cm × 7mm (55in × ¼in) wide pink satin; ribbon; 100cm × 2.5cm (39in × 1in) wide pink satin ribbon; very narrow elastic and bodkin; 3 small press fasteners; 5 small buttons. Petticoat – 20cm × 74cm (8in × 29in) white fabric; narrow white bias binding; 120cm (47in) pre-gathered white lace; 2 small press fasteners; sewing threads to match all fabrics and yarn*

Cut out all pattern pieces. Arrows indicate straight of fabric. Before cutting front head press interfacing to wrong side of calico with a warm iron. Also cut from print fabric, dress skirt 21cm × 70cm (8in × 28in) and from white fabric, petticoat skirt 19cm × 60cm (7in × 24in).

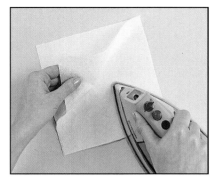

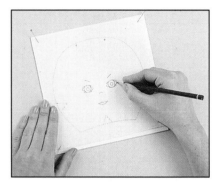

Trace front head features and place tracing onto front head fabric. To mark features onto fabric, prick through paper with a sharp pencil point and lightly draw the outlines or use dressmakers' carbon.

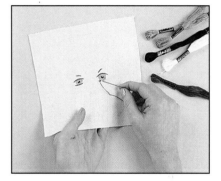

Embroider features with two strands of embroidery thread. Use satin stitch for blue eye and black centre. Brown stem stitches outline eyes and form eyebrows. Two tiny white straight stitches make a highlight in eye centres and two longer white stitches in a V-shape mark outer eyes.

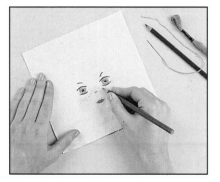

Work the mouth and nose in pink stem stitches. Lightly rub pink crayon onto fabric to colour cheeks and above nose. Colour inside mouth pink. Mark brown crayon dots for freckles. Cut out front head, stitch darts and clip open. Stitch back heads together A–U–B.

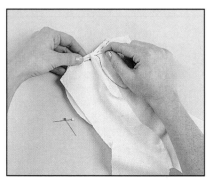

Stitch back bodies together B–C, leaving open between dots. Stitch back head to back body D–B–D. Stitch front head to front body D–D. Stitch front head and body to back head and body, around side seams and head, E–F–D–A–D–F–E leaving open lower edges of legs and inside leg seams H–C–H.

Cut 15cm (6in) of 6cm (2in) wide lace for each sock. Place wrong side of lace to right side of leg and baste lace to fabric around raw edges. Stitch upper edge of lace across legs on broken lines. Trim lace to curved edges of front legs H–G–E.

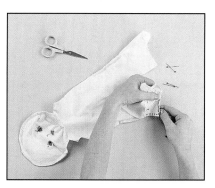

Stitch shoes to legs matching H–G–E–J–H. Stitch the short edges of the shoes together H–L. Stitch shoe soles into shoes K–Z. Stitch inside leg seams H–C–H.

Turn body through to right side, easing out legs and head. Press fabric if necessary. Fill head with stuffing, moulding it into cheeks and chin. Complete filling body and legs leaving a gap in stuffing at top of legs to allow them to bend.

Ladder stitch open edges together to enclose filling. Machine stitch around shoe straps close to edges. Sew straps around upper edges of shoes with ends to side seam of body. Sew button to overlapped ends.

Stitch darts in inner arms, remembering to reverse one arm. Stitch arms together in pairs leaving open P–Q–N. Turn through to right side easing seam around hand. Fill arm lightly with stuffing.

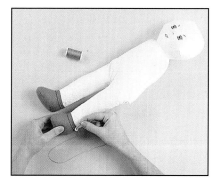

Fold upper arm at Q and inner arm at Q bringing together P–N, turn in raw edges and oversew together. To mark fingers and thumb, stab stitch through fabric and filling on broken lines, taking needle vertically through arm.

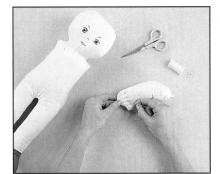

Firmly sew arms, with thumbs to front, to body side seams between dots.

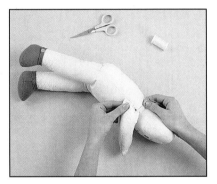

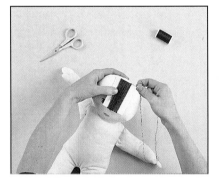

For the hair fringe, cut a piece of stiff card 5cm × 7.5cm (2in × 3in). Wind 22 strands of yarn around longer measurement. Hold short edge of card to centre seam of head with yarn to front. Sew folds of loops to fabric before sliding them off card.

Cut remaining yarn into strands 74cm (29in) long. Turn under the ends of brown tape to neaten. Stitch centre of strands to tape to form a centre parting. Place one end of tape onto front head at M and other end to the back head seam at U.

Sew tape to head. Gather yarn into two bunches at front of head and sew with brown yarn to sides of head at triangles. Trim hair.

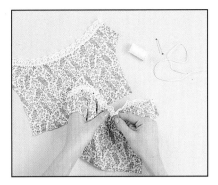

Stitch narrow hems at leg edges of pants S–S. Stitch decorative lace to right side of legs over hem stitches. Cut 15cm (6in) elastic for each leg. On wrong side place one end of elastic to edge of pant piece at placement line. Stitch through elastic stretching it as it is stitched.

Stitch both pant pieces together at one centre seam only O–R. Press a 13mm (½in) double hem to wrong side at upper edge. Stitch both edges of hem to form a channel for the elastic.

Thread through elastic, sew one end to secure and pull up to fit doll's waist. Sew other end to fabric and cut off excess. Stitch remaining centre seam O–R and inside leg seam S–R–S.

To trim dress front bodice, cut 8cm (3in) of decorative lace and 8cm (3in) of 2.5cm (1in) wide ribbon. Stitch ribbon across lower edge of panel with the lace above it.

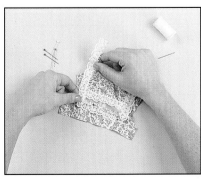

Cut and baste decorative lace around panel, folding the corners and covering raw edges of the first ribbon and lace. Stitch in place.

Stitch front bodice to back bodices at shoulders V–X. Stitch narrow hems to wrong side at centre backs. With wrong sides facing press dress neck binding along centre length, fold in raw edges to centre and press.

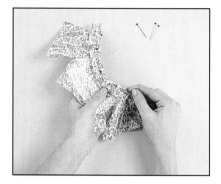

With right sides facing and raw edges even, place binding around neck edge. Stitch along fold nearest to edge. Fold binding to wrong side, turn in ends to neaten and hem binding to previous stitches.

Hem lower edge of sleeves T–T. Stitch decorative lace to right side over hem stitches and 13cm (5in) elastic to wrong side on broken lines in the same way as for the pants.

Sew a line of long running stitches to gather the top of sleeves between dots. Pull up gathers to fit and stitch sleeves into bodice arm holes W–X–W. Stitch under arm and bodice seams T–W–Y.

Press 4cm (1⅝in) to wrong side of one long edge of skirt, turn under 1cm (⅜in) and stitch hem. On right side stitch a band of 7mm (¼in) ribbon just below hem stitches with decorative lace above it.

Stitch narrow 6cm (2in) long hems at waist ends of both short sides of skirt for centre back opening. Sew a line of long running stitches close to raw edge of long side to gather it, pull up skirt to fit lower edge of bodice.

With right sides facing and gathers evenly spaced, stitch skirt to bodice. Neaten seam and press to bodice. Lap right over left at centre back and sew on press fasteners. Sew buttons on right half of bodice on top.

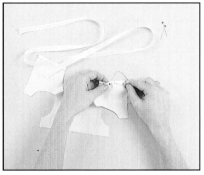

Stitch petticoat bodice front to backs at shoulders. Hem centre backs. Bind neck and arm holes with bias binding. Stitch a narrow hem at lower edge of skirt.

Stitch one length of gathered lace to hem edge and a second length to right side above hem. Complete skirt and bodice in the same way as the dress, omitting sleeves and using two press fasteners to close bodice back.

Fit clothes onto doll and tie a 2.5cm (1in) ribbon sash around waist. Cut 2cm × 36cm (¾in × 14in) narrow ribbons and tie around hair bunches.

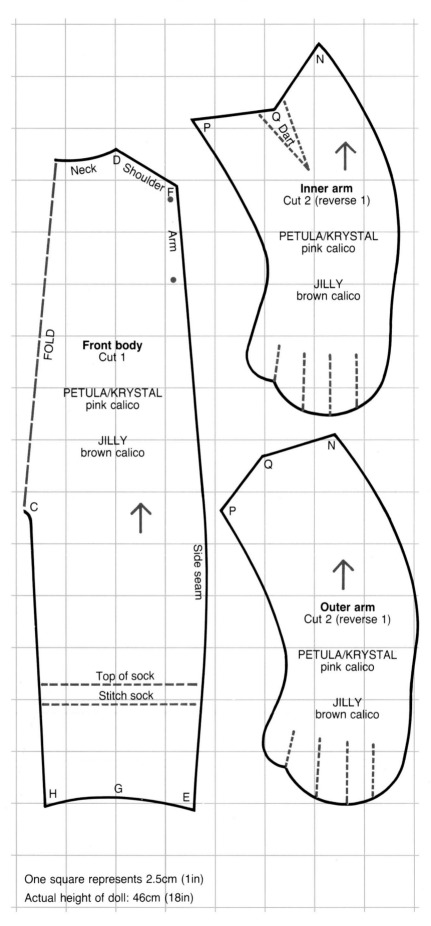

Neck

D Shoulder

Arm

FOLD

Front body
Cut 1

PETULA/KRYSTAL
pink calico

JILLY
brown calico

C

Side seam

Top of sock

Stitch sock

H   G   E

N

P   Q Dart

Inner arm
Cut 2 (reverse 1)

PETULA/KRYSTAL
pink calico

JILLY
brown calico

Q   N

P

Outer arm
Cut 2 (reverse 1)

PETULA/KRYSTAL
pink calico

JILLY
brown calico

One square represents 2.5cm (1in)
Actual height of doll: 46cm (18in)

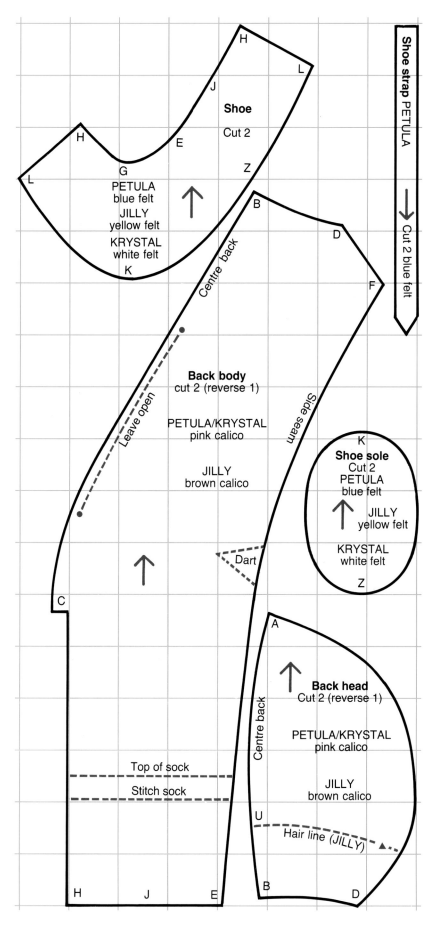

Shoe strap PETULA

Cut 2 blue felt

Shoe
Cut 2

H L J E Z G H
PETULA
blue felt
JILLY
yellow felt
KRYSTAL
white felt
K

B D F

Centre back

Back body
cut 2 (reverse 1)

PETULA/KRYSTAL
pink calico

JILLY
brown calico

Leave open

Side seam

K
Shoe sole
Cut 2
PETULA
blue felt
JILLY
yellow felt
KRYSTAL
white felt
Z

Dart

C

A
Back head
Cut 2 (reverse 1)

PETULA/KRYSTAL
pink calico

JILLY
brown calico

Centre back

U
Hair line (JILLY)

Top of sock
Stitch sock

H J E B D

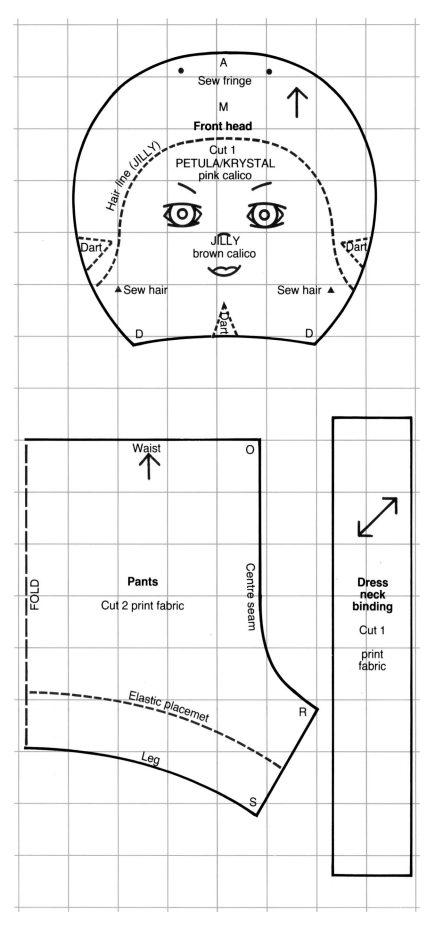

A
Sew fringe
M
Front head
Cut 1
PETULA/KRYSTAL
pink calico
Hair-line (JILLY)
JILLY
brown calico
Dart
Dart
Sew hair
Sew hair
Dart
D
D

Waist
O
FOLD
Pants
Cut 2 print fabric
Centre seam
Elastic placemet
R
Leg
S

Dress neck binding
Cut 1
print fabric

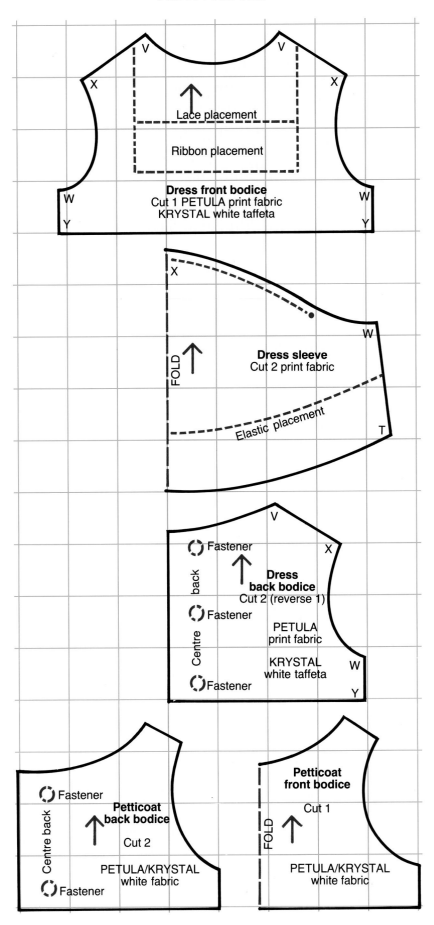

V V
X X

Lace placement

Ribbon placement

Dress front bodice
Cut 1 PETULA print fabric
KRYSTAL white taffeta

W W
Y Y

X

FOLD

Dress sleeve
Cut 2 print fabric

W

Elastic placement

T

V

⟳ Fastener

X

Dress back bodice
Cut 2 (reverse 1)

PETULA print fabric

KRYSTAL white taffeta

⟳ Fastener

Centre back

⟳ Fastener

W
Y

⟳ Fastener

Petticoat back bodice
Cut 2

Centre back

PETULA/KRYSTAL white fabric

⟳ Fastener

Petticoat front bodice
Cut 1

FOLD

PETULA/KRYSTAL white fabric

MATERIALS: *Body – 40cm × 90cm (16in × 36in) brown calico; 18cm × 18cm (7in × 7in) lightweight interfacing; 18cm × 18cm (7in × 7in) tracing paper; 23cm × 23cm (9in × 9in) yellow felt; 80cm (31in) white cord braid; 50g (1½oz) ball brown 4-ply knitting yarn; 50cm (20in) narrow striped ribbon; light brown, dark brown, black, white and red stranded embroidery threads; red crayon; filling. Track suit – 40cm × 100cm (16in × 39in) blue fleecy fabric; 100cm × 7mm (39in × ¼in) wide white ribbon; 100cm (39in) narrow yellow cord braid; narrow elastic and bodkin; 13cm (5in) white nylon press and fix fastening (Velcro); small motif. Vest – 18cm × 40cm (7in × 16in) yellow stretch fabric; 60cm × 2.5cm (24in × 1in) wide blue bias binding; 3 small press fasteners; sewing threads to match all fabrics and the yarn*

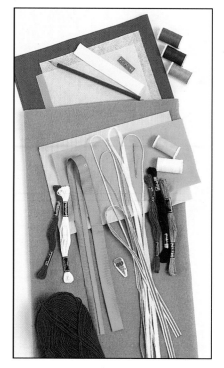

Cut out all pieces. **Note:** Omit shoe strap – this is for Petula only.

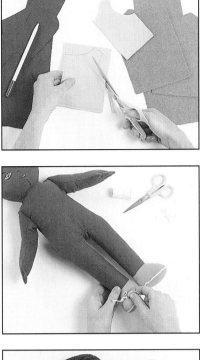

Follow steps 2–12 of the Petula instructions using light brown stranded thread in place of blue thread for the eyes and omitting lace socks. Sew white cord around shoe sole with joins at shoe seam. Sew cord bows to front of shoes.

Cut yarn into 75cm (30in) lengths. Make a light pencil mark around head on hair placement line. Keep 20 strands for curls. Place strands to head with centre of each on hair line. One end of yarn will cover face as you sew.

Continue sewing strands around back of head on placement line, leaving no gaps. Hold doll upside-down, smooth and gather strands into a pony tail hair style and tie close to head with yarn. Wind each of the 20 strands around two fingers to form loops.

Sew centre of loops around front hair line. Trim pony tail and tie with striped ribbon.

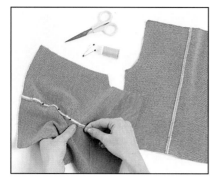

Cut 2 × 32cm (13in) lengths of white ribbon and place on fold lines of trousers. Stitch both edges of ribbon. Cut and stitch yellow braid to centre of ribbon. Stitch trouser pieces together at one centre seam only, O–R. Machine, using zig-zag or overlock stitch, raw edges at waist O–O and leg edges S–S to prevent fraying.

Fold and stitch 1.5cm (⅝in) single hem to wrong side at waist and ankles to form channels for elastic.

Thread elastic and sew one end of each to fabric at ends of channels. Pull up elastic to fit waist and ankles, sew other end of each to secure and cut off excess.

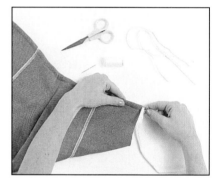

Stitch remaining centre seam O–R, including elastic. Stitch inside leg seams S–R–S. Turn trousers through to right side.

Stitch track suit top fronts to top back at shoulders T–V. Stitch ribbon and braid to the centre of sleeves on fold line as for trousers. At wrist stitch a channel and thread elastic to fit as for waist and ankles.

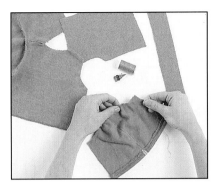

Sew long running stitches around sleeve head between dots.

Pull up gathers to fit and stitch sleeves into armholes W–V–W. Stitch underarm and side seams Y–W–X. Stitch motif to top left front. Neaten raw edges and baste 2cm (¾in) to wrong side at centre fronts. With right sides facing and raw edges even stitch one long edge of neck binding to top neck.

Turn binding over raw edges to wrong side. Turn in edges of binding to neaten, and slip stitch short edges together and long edge over previous stitches.

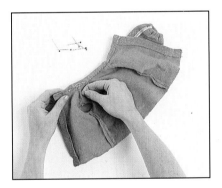

Stitch a channel at waist as for trousers. Thread through elastic and pull up to fit doll over the trousers. Machine stitch ends of elastic through fabric to secure.

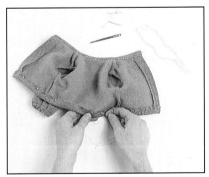

Cut the press and fix fastening in half along its length and discard one half of each piece. On left front of track suit top stitch soft piece of fastening to outside of fabric, from below neck band to lower edge. Stitch corresponding fastening to inside of right front.

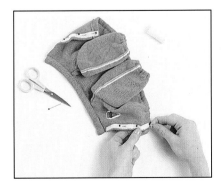

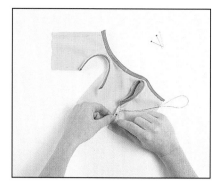

Stitch vest front to vest backs at shoulders. Stitch narrow hems to wrong side at centre backs. Bind neck and arm hole edges. Stitch side seams and a hem to wrong side at lower edge.

Sew three press fasteners, one at neck, one in centre and one at lower edge to close back. Fit cloths onto doll.

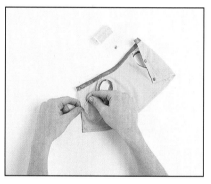

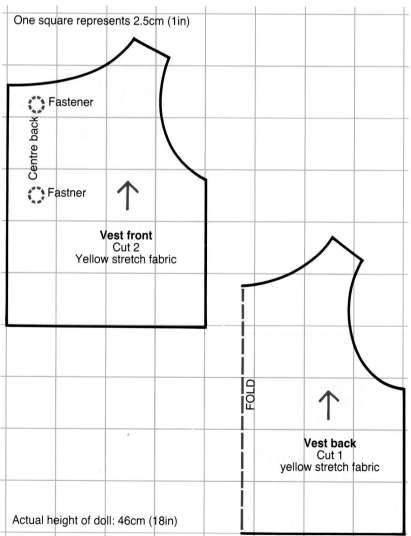

One square represents 2.5cm (1in)

Fastener

Centre back

Fastner

Vest front
Cut 2
Yellow stretch fabric

FOLD

Vest back
Cut 1
yellow stretch fabric

Actual height of doll: 46cm (18in)

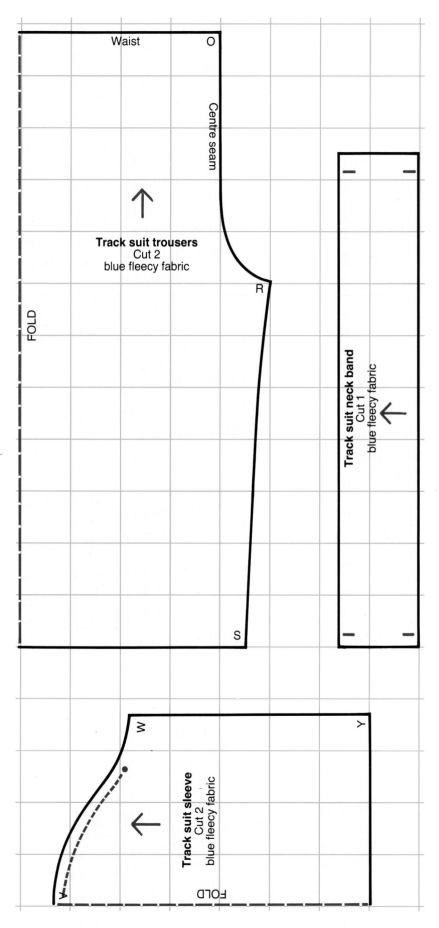

Waist — O

Centre seam

Track suit trousers
Cut 2
blue fleecy fabric

FOLD

R

S

Track suit neck band
Cut 1
blue fleecy fabric

W

Y

Track suit sleeve
Cut 2
blue fleecy fabric

A

FOLD

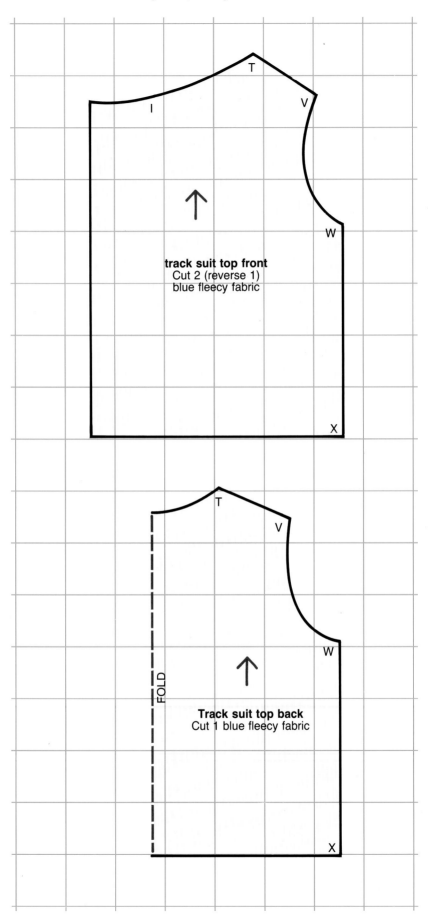

track suit top front
Cut 2 (reverse 1)
blue fleecy fabric

Track suit top back
Cut 1 blue fleecy fabric

FOLD

KRYSTAL, THE SNOW QUEEN

MATERIALS: Body – 40cm × 90cm (16in × 36in) pink calico; 18cm × 18cm (7in × 7in) lightweight stretch interfacing; 18cm × 18cm (7in × 7in) tracing paper; 23cm × 23cm (9in × 9in) white felt; 60cm × 1cm (24in × 3/8in) wide silver ribbon; 50g (1½oz) ball cream 4-ply knitting yarn; 16cm (6in) cream tape; pale blue, black, white, light brown and pale pink stranded embroidery silks; pale pink crayon; 95cm (37in) small pearl type beads; 5cm × 7cm (2in × 2¾in) stiff card; clear drying craft glue; filling. Dress and pantaloons – 70cm × 114cm (28in × 45in) white taffeta fabric; 220cm (87in) narrow lace; 260cm (102in) silver braid; 150cm × 24mm (59in × 7/8in) wide white ribbon; very narrow elastic and bodkin; 3 small press fasteners; 3 small buttons. Petticoat – 30cm × 90cm (12in × 36in) white cotton fabric; 140cm (55in) narrow lace; narrow white bias binding; 2 small press fasteners. Cloak – 20cm × 100cm (8in × 39in) white fleece fabric; 20cm × 100cm (8in × 39in) silver lining fabric; 6cm × 140cm (2in × 55in) short pile white fur fabric (cut across width of fabric); 100cm × 13mm (39in × ½in) white ribbon; sewing threads to match all fabrics and yarn

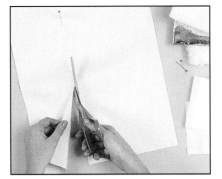

Cut out all pattern pieces. Use taffeta for dress and pantaloons and white cotton fabric for petticoat. Arrows indicate straight of fabric. Also cut from white taffeta dress skirt 20cm × 70cm (8in × 28in) and dress skirt frill 11cm × 114cm (4in × 45in). From white fabric, petticoat skirt 28cm × 70cm (11in × 28in). Cut one complete cloak from fleece fabric and one complete lining.

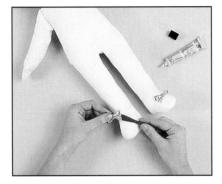

Follow steps 2–12 of the Petula instructions using pale blue stranded thread for the eye. Tie small silver ribbon bows and sew to front of shoes.

The hair is made in same way as Petula but do not tie it into two bunches. To hold hair to head use a needle and yarn to make a stitch at one side seam of head on triangle, take yarn across all hair and make a second stitch on centre back seam at U. Pull yarn to bring hair close to head. Repeat for remaining hair.

Make several stitches across hair. Cut three lengths of pearl beads each 25cm (10in) long, hold ends together and tie with thread. Twist strands and sew ends to head under front hair line. Secure beads around head with stitches taken through head.

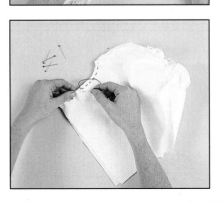

Follow Petula steps 16–18 noting that pantaloons for Krystal have long legs and lace is straight. Follow Petula steps 21 and 22. Stitch lace around neck with silver braid above it.

To form a channel for wrist elastic, fold a 2cm (¾in) hem to wrong side of sleeve T–T. Turn under raw edge and stitch hem. On right side stitch one length of lace to edge of sleeve and a second length on hem stitches, taking care not to block channel. Stitch silver braid across sleeve above lace.

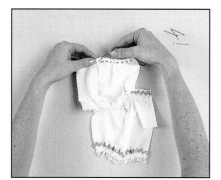

Thread elastic and sew one end to fabric, pull up to fit wrist and secure other end. Trim excess elastic. Sew a line of long running stitches to gather top of sleeves between dots. Pull up gathers to fit and stitch sleeves into arm holes W–X–W. Stitch underarm and bodice seams T–W–Y.

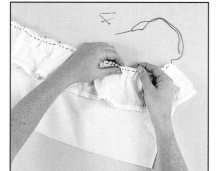

Stitch a narrow hem to one long edge of skirt frill. On right side stitch straight edge of lace over hem stitches, and silver braid above lace. Sew long running stitches to gather opposite long edge of frill. Pull up stitches and with right sides together and raw edges even sew frill to one long edge of skirt.

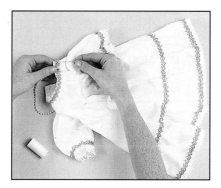

Press seam to skirt and sew silver braid to right side over seam. Refer to Petula steps 26 and 27. Sew end of remaining 20cm (8in) pearl beads to each end of neck band. Follow Petula steps 28 and 29 noting that petticoat skirt is longer and only one length of straight lace is stitched to right side of hem.

Using white fleece stitch cloak fronts to cloak back AA–BB. Stitch darts at hood neck. Stitch hood seam CC–DD. Stitch hood to cloak neck M–M matching dots at centre back. Make up lining in same way. With right sides facing stitch cloak and hood to lining around all edges leaving a gap open at lower back between triangles.

Turn to right side out through gap, fold raw edges to inside and slip stitch together. Catch stitch fabrics together around neck. To make trimming use 6cm × 140cm (2in × 55in) fur fabric. With wrong sides facing fold it along centre length, turn in raw edges and sew together.

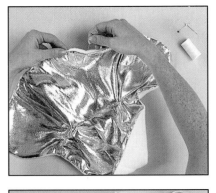

Beginning at lower centre back, sew fur trimming to fleece around cloak and hood, keeping fur edges to fabric. To join ends of trimming, open them out and sew both pieces together across width, refold and sew in place. Cut 1cm (⅜in) wide ribbon into two pieces and sew at M on neck seams. Fit clothes onto doll and tie 2.5cm (1in) ribbon sash around waist.

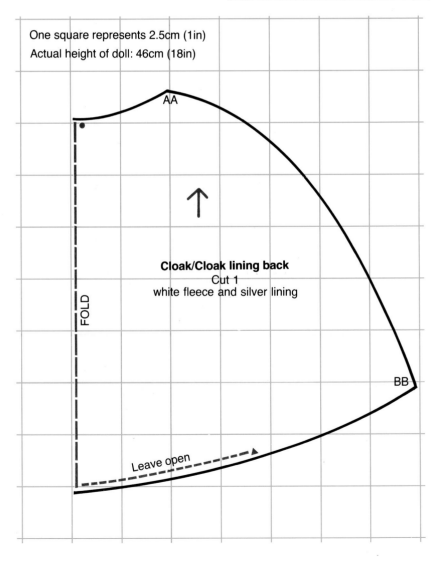

One square represents 2.5cm (1in)
Actual height of doll: 46cm (18in)

AA

↑

Cloak/Cloak lining back
Cut 1
white fleece and silver lining

FOLD

BB

Leave open

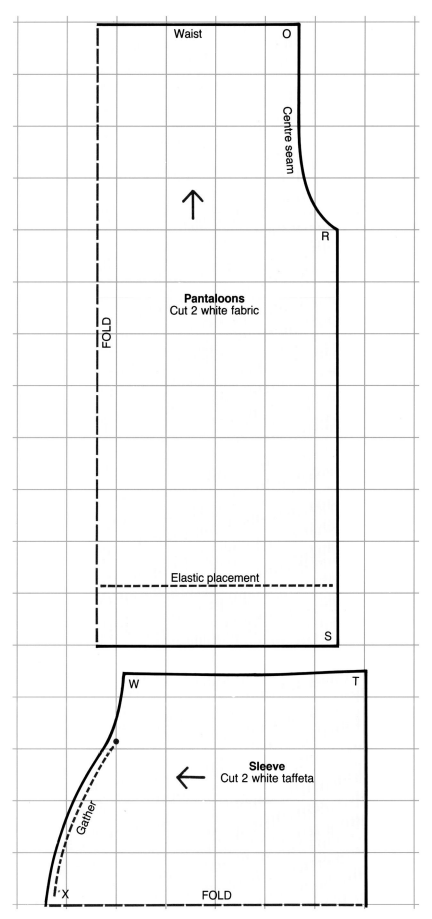

Waist

O

Centre seam

R

Pantaloons
Cut 2 white fabric

FOLD

Elastic placement

S

W

T

Sleeve
Cut 2 white taffeta

Gather

X

FOLD

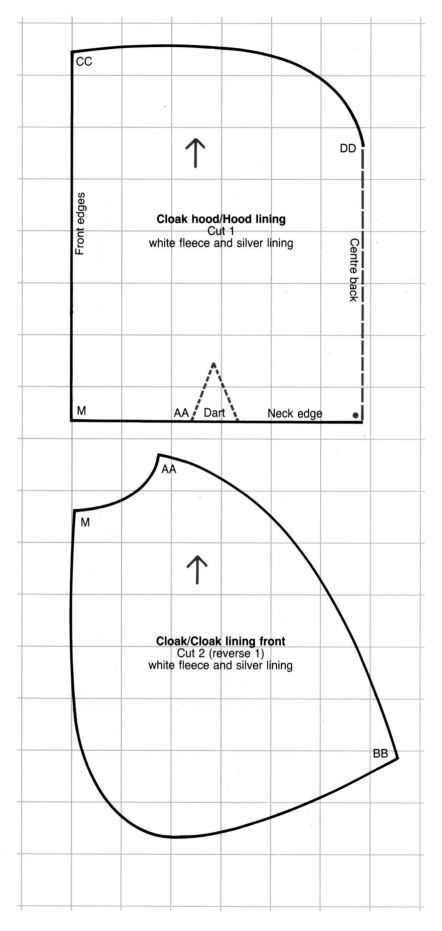

CC

DD

↑

Front edges

Cloak hood/Hood lining
Cut 1
white fleece and silver lining

Centre back

M   AA   Dart   Neck edge

AA

M

↑

Cloak/Cloak lining front
Cut 2 (reverse 1)
white fleece and silver lining

BB

YARN DOLLS

MATERIALS: Small amounts of yarn in main colour and brown; scraps of red and black felts; ribbon or lace for trimming; clear drying adhesive; stiff card; paper punch; tweezers

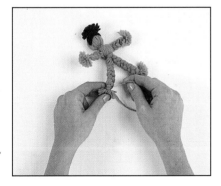

The yarn strands are cut extra long to allow for easier manipulation and then trimmed. The yarn for all bindings is wound four times around body or limbs. The ends are then tied or threaded into doll with a needle to secure them on one side of doll. That side will then become doll's back. Any ribbon or lace must be sewn on firmly.

To make either doll: For the body cut 60 strands of main colour yarn each 36cm (14in) long. For easy even measurement, cut a piece of stiff card 18cm × 6cm (7in × 2½in), wind yarn 60 times around longer length and cut through all strands at one point.

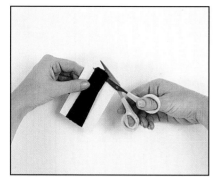

For the boy's hair: Cut 30 strands of brown yarn each 20cm (8in). Again this can be done by cutting card 10cm × 6cm (4in × 2½in), wind 30 strands around longer length and cut through at one point. **For the girl's hair:** Cut 20 strands each 30cm (11¾in). A piece of card 15cm × 6cm (6in × 2½in) can be used, wind 20 strands around longer length and cut through at one point.

For either doll: Place hair strands across centre of body strands and fold body strands over hair pieces. The smooth fold of the body strands which covers the hair will become the doll's face. Wind a piece of yarn several times around body just below hair to form neck and fasten yarn at back of toy.

For either doll: Bring the hair strands together above the head with ends even. Wind brown yarn around hair close to head. **For the boy:** Trim the hair to 1cm (⅜in) above the binding. **For the girl:** Spread a thin layer of glue onto back and sides of head. Allow glue to dry slightly then arrange hair to cover head and trim ends of yarn.

For either doll: To make arms cut 51 strands of main colour yarn each 24cm (9in) long. Holding strands together with ends even bind them tightly at 2cm (¾in) from one end to form a wrist.

Divide the strands into three groups of 17. Plait strands evenly to a length of 9cm (3½in) from the previous binding. Bind around plait for the second wrist and trim both ends 8mm ($^{3/16}$in) from the bindings to make hands.

For either doll: With the face to the front, divide body strands into two groups and place arms between them with a hand to each side. Bind around body pieces under arms.

For the boy: Divide lower strands of body piece into two groups to make legs. Separate each group into three sections of 20 strands. Plait the leg for 5cm (2in) from the body binding. Bind all strands for the end of leg and trim foot strands to be slightly longer than hands.

For the girl: The yarn strands below the waist binding are left loose to form the doll's skirt. Cut strands to make a doll of 12cm (5in) in height.

Use the paper punch to cut from felt two black circles and one red circle. To make eyes and mouth, cut each circle across centre and use half of each for the features. Glue eyes to head with the curved edges upwards and the mouth in place with the curved edge downwards.

For the boy: Tie a tiny ribbon bow and sew to front neck. **For the girl:** Tie a ribbon sash around the waist or make a hair bow. Ribbon can also be folded across the chest as a bodice. Sew a scrap of lace at girl doll's neck or waist.

INDEX

ACKNOWLEDGMENTS

The author and publisher wish to thank the following for their help in supplying materials for the book. These firms provide a mail order service to supply a wide range of soft doll, toy and craft materials (catalogues available):

Beckfoot Mill, Prince Street, Dudley Hill, Bradford, West Yorkshire BD4 6HQ. Supply fillings, doll fabrics, Christmas fabrics, felts, 'cotton balls'.

Ridings Craft, 749 Bradford Road, Batley, West Yorkshire WF17 8HZ. Specialize in doll accessories, fabrics, lace and trimmings.

Fred Aldous Ltd., P.O. Box 135, Lever Street, Manchester M60 1UX. Amongst a vast range of craft materials, supplies felts, pipe cleaners, dolls' faces, 'cotton balls'.